MOTHERS IN PRISON

MOTHERS IN PRISON

PHYLLIS JO BAUNACH

Transaction Books
New Brunswick (U.S.A.) and Oxford (U.K.)

Library of Congress Catalog Number: 84-16162
ISBN: 0-88738-027-1 (cloth)
Printed in the United States of America

Library of Congress Cataloging in Publication Data

Baunach, Phyllis Jo.
  Mothers in prison.

  Bibliography: p.
  Includes index.
  1. Women prisoners—United States—Case studies.   2. Mothers—United States—Case studies.   3. Maternal deprivation—Case studies.   I. Title.
HV9471.B39   1985   365'.43   84-16162
ISBN 0-88738-027-1

Contents

For inmate-mothers everywhere, who know the pain of separation from children

For my mother, Josephine Baunach, who first showed me love

For Eddie, Caroline and Helen, parents who care

For Thomas O. Murton, who guided my career

and

For Randy Knack, my patient husband

"For me, the biggest problem of being a mother in prison is that I can't care for my children. You can write to them and maybe talk on the phone. But you can't make decisions for them; you are stripped of it. You are not a mother in prison!"

—An inmate-mother

List of Tables

Acknowledgments

This project could not have been completed without the support, assistance, and cooperation of many people. My sincerest appreciation to the National Institute of Justice (NIJ) for sponsorship of the project. In particular, Blair Ewing, former acting director of the NIJ, along with Carolyn Burstein, former NIJ staff member, guided the creation of the In-House Research Program and had faith in me as one of two staff members to make it work the first year. Betty Chemers, special assistant to the director, Robert Burkhart, director of the Office of Research Programs (ORP), Ann Schmidt, special assistant to the director of ORP, Carrie Smith, administrative officer, and Philip Merrils, former contracts specialist, provided important administrative services which kept the project alive. John Spevacek, my former supervisor and project monitor served as a liaison with the NIJ and supported my efforts throughout the year.

Peter Lejins, professor emeritus and former chairman gave the project a home in the Institute of Criminal Justice and Criminology at the University of Maryland. Mary Jean Wood, assistant research faculty member during the study, carefully attended to administrative matters for the project at the university. I am grateful to Professors Peter Maida and William Minor for testing out ideas with me for the study.

I would also like to express my sincerest appreciation to administrators and institutional personnel in Kentucky and Washington state for their cooperation and assistance throughout the project. Dr. David Bland, former commissioner of corrections in Kentucky, encouraged me to pursue the study in his home state. Within the Bureau of Corrections, Pat Ray Reese, manager of the Systems Maintenance Unit at the time of the study, arranged for clearances in Kentucky's two correctional institutions for women and provided useful comments in the development of the data collection instruments.

In Washington state, Robert Sharpley, executive secretary for the Department of Social and Health Service (DSHS) Human Research Review Section assisted me in working through appropriate channels to obtain approval for the study, and Mr. Robert Tropp, former director of DSHS authorized the study in Washington's womens' prison.

Superintendents Betty Kassulke of the Kentucky Correctional Institution for Women (KCIW), James Lenhoff of the Daniel Boone Career Development Center (DBCDC) and Sue Clark of the Purdy Treatment Center (PTC) for Women in Washington and Nancy Cook, acting superintendent of the DBCDC each provided me total access to their institutions and complete cooperation in every way.

A special note of appreciation goes to the staff members of each institution for tolerating incessant questions about the separation of and programs for inmate-mothers and their children. In particular, Jane Thompson, academic principal and Chaplain John Lentz at KCIW and Jim Carey and the drug and alcohol counselors at PTC shared their offices as interview sites and their thoughts about mothering from prisons. Frankie Beasley, director of the Mother Offspring Life Development Program (MOLD) at DBCDC, Roberta Chapman, former home economics and child development teacher, Kathy Farmer, nursery school teacher, Dorene Buckles, former diagnostic administrator, and Dick Theroux, former clinical social worker and family therapist at PTC offered their philosophies and insights regarding mechanisms for imprisoned mothers to maintain ties with their children. Nancy Nash and Diane Waddington, childcare careworkers for the Department of Social and Health Services and Dick Theroux provided perspectives on foster parents in Pierce and Kitsap counties in Washington state.

The data for this project would have been incomplete without the patient and competent assistance of Ms. Vaughn and Jimmie Larsen and the staff members of the records sections in Kentucky and Washington states, respectively. Travis Fritsch gave me permission to use some of the questions she had devised for another survey.

I would especially like to acknowledge Dr. Rita Warren, whose advice and constructive criticism contributed to the development of the taped interviews.

Data analysis was carried out through the facilities and partial support of the Computer Science Center at the University of Maryland. I am indebted to the persistent and diligent efforts of Doug Mayer, a former graduate student at the Institute of Criminal Justice and Criminology, and Thomas Tugman, a consultant at the Computer Science Center, in tackling the problems associated with the analysis of a large data base. Two other capable students at the Institute of Criminal Justice and Criminology bear recognition. Debbie Higgins spent the spring and summer of 1979 in coding data and Mary Parsons listened to hours of tapes.

The production of this book could not have been completed without the able assistance of many others. Dr. Irving Louis Horowitz and Scott Bramson encouraged and guided revisions of earlier versions. The profesional skill of Dalia Buzin, my editor, helped a great deal in polishing the final draft. Bob Elwood provided technical expertise in preparing the final manuscript for publication. Julia Perkins and Jean Magnotto spent endless hours in diligently and patiently typing and retyping the drafts.

My very special appreciation to the respondents in this study. Foster parents in Washington state opened up their homes as well as their thoughts to a total stranger. Finally and most importantly, the women in prison who let me into their world have given me a better understanding of them, their concerns about children, and the burdens they endure as incarcerated women, and especially, as mothers.

Preface

This project was undertaken as part of an In-House Research Program sponsored by the National Institute of Justice (NIJ), U.S. Department of Justice. Begun in 1977, the program enables staff members of the NIJ to take up to one year's leave of absence from their regular responsibilities to pursue a research project of their own design.

The literature regarding the separation of inmate-mothers from their children consistently recommends the development of programs or mechanisms to assist inmate-mothers to maintain ties with their children during incarceration. At the time this project was begun, there were programs of this nature in at least four states: Washington, Kentucky, Minnesota, and Nebraska. However, with the exception of occasional newspaper or magazine articles, to date there has been little research documenting the background, development, implementation, operations, or residents' perceptions of these programs for inmate-mothers and their children. Thus, one of the objectives of the current project was to provide a brief descriptive analysis of programs in two institutions. The institutions selected for study included the Daniel Boone Career Development Center (DBCDC) in Kentucky and the Purdy Treatment Center for Women (PTC) in Washington state. These states were selected on the basis of accessibility, interest in the project, and the stage of program development.

A second objective was to explore imprisoned mothers' perceptions of the separation from their children and its effect on them, their children, and the relationship. For this objective, mothers in three prisons were interviewed. These prisons included two in Kentucky and one in Washington state. Questions were raised regarding inmate-mothers' perceptions of mothering skills; attitudes towards parenting; level of confidence in resuming maternal responsibilities and self-concept; demographic and situational characteristics of children (for example, living situation prior to mother's incarceration, current caretaker, mother's satsifaction with current caretaker, number of placements and caretakers since mother's incarceration, who has legal custody); perceived problems children have encountered since mother's incarceration; perception of children's knowledge of mother's current living arrangements and who informed them; and where children were at various points in the criminal justice process.

At one of the sites selected for study, the Purdy Treatment Center for Women, there is a program to place children in foster care near the institution. Thus, a third objective was to ascertain from foster parents their perceptions of their roles and responsibilities towards children and imprisoned mothers.

As an exploratory study, several questions rather than specific hypotheses guided the research. In this sense, the study was intended as an hypothesis-generating as opposed to an hypothesis-testing effort.

The methodology for the study consisted of interviews with residents, in prisons in two states, both mothers and nonmothers, and with a small number of staff in the institutions in which there were programs for imprisoned mothers and their children. Administrators and staff were interviewed to obtain information about the development, implementation, and operation of programs. Interviews were conducted during the spring and summer of 1979.

Some of the findings regarding the impacts of the separation indicate that:

> Children lived most often with their mothers prior to incarceration. The current separation is the first major separation for most children from their mothers.

> Most mothers retain legal custody of their children or have relinquished custody temporarily during incarceration. In addition, mothers generally want to live with children following release. Mothers thus consider the separation as temporary.

> Mothers generally want to maintain ties with children and employ the means available. These means generally include letters, phone calls, and to a lesser extent, visits or furloughs.

> Mothers often noted that the separation exacerbated or brought about emotional, physical, or academic problems for their children. In addition, mothers report that they will have adjustment problems in resuming maternal responsibilities.

> Despite feelings of guilt about the reasons for the separation, mothers themselves have usually told children that they are in prison. However, they may have been unable to relate the real reasons for the separation at the outset.

As more women come before the bar of justice and presumably as more mothers are incarcerated, there will remain a need for ways to handle the problems of the separation. As an hypothesis-generating effort, it is hoped that this study will stimulate additional research and subsequent programmatic development in this significant yet neglected area.

This project was supported by Order Number 8-0754-J-LEAA awarded by the Law Enforcement Assistance Administration, U.S. Department of Justice, under the Omnibus Crime Control and Safe Streets Act of 1968, as amended. Points of view or opinions stated in this document are those of the author and do not necessarily represent the official position or policies of the U.S. Department of Justice, the National Institute of Justice, the Bureau of Justice Statistics, or the University of Maryland.

1

The Separation Impacts: Common Threads
from Previous Research

One of most significant problems confronting incarcerated women in this country is the loss of their loved ones, particularly their children (Ward and Kassenbaum 1966; Burkhart 1973; Baunach and Murton 1973; Baunach 1975). This problem is especially acute since between 50 percent and 70 percent of incarcerated women have one or more dependent children who were living with them prior to their imprisonment.[1] Moreover, the average number of children for each inmate-mother is between two and three (McGowan and Blumenthal 1978; Zalba 1964; Bonfanti et al. 1974), and many of the incarcerated women have children younger than thirteen. This concern may seem ironic in a time when women are striving to replace the role of housewife and mother with more professional ventures. Yet, considering that most incarcerated women are poor, disproportionately from minority groups, have had little education beyond the tenth grade, have few skills, and have had virtually no prior vocational training opportunities in other than traditional female occupations, for example, clerk, cosmetologist, nurse's aid (Glick and Neto 1977), this concern may not seem so improbable.

Whatever else they had, imprisoned mothers had one thing to hang onto before their incarceration: their children. Whether the relationship was healthy or otherwise for mother and child, when a woman goes to prison she takes with her the good memories of that relationship and cherishes the times spent in sharing joy and love with her children. Perhaps she truly loved and cared for her children in a positive healthy relationship; perhaps she reversed roles with her children and they primarily nurtured her; perhaps she paid little or no attention to her children at all. In any case, imprisonment engenders the feelings of loss and failure. Not only has she been ostracized by society for her criminal behavior, she has demonstrated a seeming failure as a mother. Whatever else prison does to or for a woman, it enables her to reflect for hours on end about herself and the consequences of her behavior on both herself and her children.

1

Separation for any reason may be traumatic. A child's first day at school, hospitalization for life-saving surgery, military service, especially during wartime, or the ultimate separation, death, all entail a tremendous emotional loss. But in each of these instances there may be a higher good, a sense of inevitability, or lack of control that may be used as a comforting explanation or excuse for the separation. However, incarceration carries with it the stigma that one's own behavior, whether conscious or not, has created the reason for the separation. In this respect, a sense of guilt and bitterness overshadows the pains of imprisonment for inmate-mothers.

Should the Mother-Child Relationship Be Maintained during/following the Mother's Incarceration?

Whether or not an inmate-mother should retain or relinquish her parental rights to her children during or following incarceration involves both moral and legal decisions which in some ways may overlap. From a legal perspective, Palmer (1972) argued that incarceration, per se, does not provide adequate evidence that a parent is unfit. Rather, he suggested, the courts should consider additional factors such as the woman's relationship to the offspring prior to incarceration and the causal relationship between the criminal act and the mother's ability to perform her parental role. With these points in mind, judges would be better able to determine the mother's parental fitness and to decide whether or not the children should be placed in her custody after her release.

Another argument along these lines was that legislative guidelines limit the extent to which the courts may modify their procedures for deciding parental fitness. Guidelines currently consider the best interests of the children, but simultaneously treat the issue of parental fitness inequitably. Established standards such as nonsupport, child abuse, neglect, desertion, drunkenness, adultery, mental illness, and incarceration, have been regarded as manifestations of the abandonment of responsibilities and a justification for the termination of parental rights. Palmer pointed out that these interpretations are erroneous and that a reassessment of the standards is required (Palmer 1972:134).

The court's consideration of a mother's criminal act and subsequent incarceration as voluntary relinquishment of her parental rights was decided in *In re Jameson* (1967). In this case, the court held that the mother knew prior to committing the act that she would be incarcerated for it if convicted. Palmer challenged this justification as illogical, since the woman's intention may have been to obtain money or food with no intention of getting caught. Furthermore, if she wished to abandon her child, the woman could have devised alternative means that would not have been detrimental or discomforting to herself.

Palmer suggested that imprisonment in and of itself does not constitute abandonment. Rather, additional factors such as parental neglect and withholding affection should be used to substantiate claims of abandonment. Given this background, he recommended legislative reform—allowing an inmate to live with her children (under two years old) in prison, in conditions conducive to a positive interaction; devising "mother release" programs to enable inmate-mothers to stay with their children in the community; and reforming visitation practices to allow for more relaxed visits in less security-oriented surroundings.

More recently, the Indiana Court of Appeals decided that although incarceration does not necessarily constitute abandonment, this possibility is not excluded. A minimum of one year of no communication between parent and child is required by law for termination of parental rights without consent. According to the National Legal Resource Center for Child Advocacy and Protection (1982:8), the court held that

> a parent's pattern of behavior which evidences an intent to abandon the child prior to his imprisonment could be deemed to persist while in prison. Under this circumstance, the pre-incarceration and incarceration periods could be combined to meet the statutory time requirement. (*Herman* v. *Arnold*, 406 N.E. 2d 277 1980.)

This decision suggests, as Palmer had earlier, that the determination of "intent" to abandon is a key factor in equating incarceration with abandonment.

In a brief review of recent court cases, the National Legal Resource Center for Child Advocacy and Protection (1982) pointed out that most courts have ruled that incarceration in and of itself is not sufficient grounds for termination of parental rights without a law that allows such termination upon conviction. Current "unfitness" remains a usual requirement for termination of parental rights. A parent convicted of a crime that may be construed as rendering him/her unfit for custody and control of the child may lose parental rights. The center further noted that the Kentucky Court of Appeals decided that an inmate parent has an "affirmative duty" to retain some ties with his/her child in order to stave off termination of parental rights during incarceration. Another court indicated that termination may be prevented if an incarcerated parent finds an appropriate home for children, for example with relatives; this effort suggests a sustained interest in the welfare of the child (National Legal Resource Center for Child Advocacy and Protection 1982:1, 8).

With respect to legislation, Shepard and Zemans (1950) found that thirteen states had statutory provisions which permitted inmate-mothers to have infant children remain in the institution with them for as long as two years.[2] Nearly half of the laws did not set a maximum time limit but suggested that children should be removed "when the health and comfort of the child require its removal,'' or ''at the discretion of the Board of Corrections'' (Shephard and Zemans 1950:18–19). Whether or not these statutes remain in force is unclear. What is clear, however, is that, with the exception of New York State, babies born to incarcerated women in this country do not usually live with them in prison.

Consequently, there has been a growing concern for the legal rights and rehabilitative needs of inmate-mothers and their children. This concern was reflected in a California law suit regarding an inmate-mother's right to have her children live with her in prison. The suit, however, was denied in court. Arguments raised included the effects that the prison environment and procedures could have on the child and the potential effects of the child's presence on the prison and other inmates (LaPoint 1977:13–14).

Similarly, in 1979 a Florida law enabled courts to grant permission for mothers to keep their babies born in prison with them if they felt it was in the child's ''best interests.'' More recently, however, this authority was diminished by an amendment to the law which gave the department of corrections more authority to determine which inmate-mothers could keep their children.

Along the same lines, the American Civil Liberties Union (ACLU) has begun to assist inmate-mothers who want to maintain close contact with their children during imprisonment. In South Carolina, the ACLU has been working with a young woman serving a 21-year sentence for armed robbery who wants to keep her child with her in prison. In Virginia, the ACLU filed a class action suit in 1983 on behalf of women in the state prison who expect to give birth during incarceration and who either gave birth while confined or immediately prior to their incarceration. The action seeks to enable inmate-mothers to remain with their infants in appropriate accommodations either on or off prison grounds (ACLU National Prison Project, personal communique, 26 August 1983). In 1983, the Connecticut Civil Liberties Union (CCLU) filed a class action suit on behalf of women incarcerated in the Connecticut Correctional Institution at Niantic. Among the issues raised in the complaint were the inadequate treatment of pregnant inmates and the inadequate visiting services and facilities for inmate-mothers and their children (CCLU, personal communique, 17 October 1983).

The extent to which inmate-mothers win the rights to have children live with them in prison has yet to be determined. The nature of the complaints noted here suggests an increasing and more vocal demand among inmate-mothers to keep babies with them during incarceration.

Effects of the Separation on the Children

Although the present study is concerned primarily with the effects of the separation on inmate-mothers, it is important to point out that there is a growing body of literature on the impacts of the separation on the children of incarcerated parents (McCord and McCord 1958; Moerk 1973; Savage 1974; LaPoint 1977; Stanton 1980). Sack et al. (1976), for instance, interviewed children, caretakers, and thirty-one White mothers and fathers incarcerated in Oregon prisons. Sixteen of twenty-two children of imprisoned fathers who were observed and later interviewed manifested some disturbances. All sixteen children indicated problems with peer relationships. Additional clinical findings suggested that the fathers' incarceration may engender frequent symptomatic behavior, especially for children in ages ranging from 5 to 14.

Robins et al. (1976) examined the effects of parental arrest on the behavior of adolescents. The authors found that children's delinquency could be predicted from parental arrest records. The only factor mediating delinquency seemed to be the number of siblings: large families were more likely to have at least one delinquent. Generally, the studies that have been completed suggest that there may be deleterious psychological effects on children of incarcerated parents. Whether or not the parents' incarceration or criminal behavior may be totally or mostly responsible for these effects, however, has not been demonstrated to date.

Studies pertaining to effects of parental incarceration on children have been mentioned here primarily to highlight concern in this area. The focus of this book is on the impact of the separation on the mothers. Lack of time and resources precluded a detailed examination of the impact of the separation on the children.

Effects of the Separation on Inmate-Mothers

As with the study of women in prison generally, there has been little research to date examining the impacts of the separation on inmate-mothers. Some studies describe the characteristics of these women, their general feelings about the separation (Bonfanti et al. 1974; DuBose 1975; Lundberg et al. 1975; McGowan and Blumenthal 1978), and the problems of coordinating agency services to meet the needs of both inmate-mothers and their children (Zalba 1964; McGowan and Blumenthal 1978). Despite the fact that each of these studies was conducted in a different state with varying numbers of inmate-mothers,[3] there are several common threads in the findings and recommendations among them. To set the stage for discussion of the present study, these themes will be discussed briefly.

Common Threads in the Findings

Commonalities in findings center on factors such as the prior living situations of mothers and children, attempts to maintain ties with children during imprisonment, planned reunions, the importance of the mothering role to these women, and limited institutional support to maintain mother-child bonds.

Prior Living Situation. A large proportion of inmate-mothers in some of the studies were reportedly living with their children prior to arrest for the current conviction.[4] However, none of the studies explored the nature of the relationship prior to the mother's arrest, nor did they verify the mother's self-reports by interviewing caretakers, other relatives, or the children. Therefore, the quality of prior relationships and the extent to which mothers actually cared for the children themselves prior to incarceration have not been determined.

Maintaining Ties During Incarceration. Many of the incarcerated women reportedly attempt to maintain contact with their children through the means available, which in most instances consists of telephone calls or correspondence with children or caretakers or visits in the prison.[5] Zalba, however, noted that nearly one-half of the children had not seen their mothers since incarceration. Of those children who had lived with their mothers prior to incarceration, nearly one-third had not visited the institution. Although responsible adults and caretakers generally recognized the importance of regular contact between inmate-mother and child, some of the caretakers reportedly expressed anger, hostility, or disapproval of the mother's criminal behavior (Zalba 1964:85). These attitudes may well account for the lack of contact between inmate-mothers and children.

The general finding that incarcerated mothers attempt to maintain contact with their children has three possible explanations. One relatively favorable explanation is that inmate-mothers may have been ''good'' mothers on the outside and may genuinely have cared for their children and, thus, may wish to maintain contact with their children during their incarceration. A second more skeptical possibility is that the women may have cared little for their children prior to arrest and may simply consider it socially desirable to express motherly concerns. They may believe that behaving in this manner will positively impress institutional personnel and parole board members, thereby influencing the decision for an early release date.

A third possibility is that, prior to their incarceration, women in prison may have been wrapped up in their own lives, perhaps to the exclusion of involvement with their children. Once in prison, however, they may have an opportunity to take a hard look at both themselves and their relationships with their children. For some women this may be the first time they have stopped to consider the effects of their own behaviors on their children's lives. These women may then feel a great deal of guilt or anger at themselves for the experiences they have put their children through. The extent of and conditions under which any of these possible explanations apply, however, have not been examined.

Planned Reunions. A substantial proportion of the inmate-mothers in each study reportedly planned to reunite with their children following release from prison and thus regarded the separation as only temporary.[6] However, resuming responsibility immediately after release may be unrealistic. Zalba (1964:117) noted that the added burden of child care so soon after release could lead to unforseeable difficulties in coping and adjustment, could seriously jeopardize the mother's rehabilitative potential while on parole, or could result in reducing the children's chances for a stable social and emotional adjustment. Similarly, Lundberg et al. (1975) pointed out that women who foresaw little or no difficulties in the reunion with their children may be unrealistically assessing the complexity of the emotions involved.

At the time of the reunion the crucial issue is the extent to which both mother and child have internalized their defenses. In the absence of resolving or working through the grief associated with the separation, the mother-child relationship might be jeopardized. Children are much more vulnerable than adults and may be subject to more severe disturbances as a result of the loss. Thus, the mother's resolution of the grief may be a significant factor in maintaining a healthy reunion and relationship with the child.

Importance of the Mothering Role. The role of mother appears to be a very important aspect of the lives of these women. Lundberg et al. (1975:36) found that the maternal role seemed to be a significant "axis of self-esteem and interpersonal feedback and definition." Based on their data, the authors surmised that "the mothers interviewed . . . perceive their role as mothers as primary to their sense of identity and view their imprisonment as a deprivation to their children" (ibid.:59). In this same context, Zalba (1964:23) had suggested earlier that the role of mother may be crucial to the inmate-mothers and that "separation from her children and the major changes in her role more directly strike at her personal identity and her self-image as a woman."

In contrast with these findings, Glick and Neto (1977:170) found that the importance of motherhood may vary with age. Older inmates (over 35) more often than younger inmates (18-21) agreed that it is important to have children, and that women who do not want children are selfish. Although these analyses did not take into account whether or not respondents had children of their own, since over half of the respondents were mothers, the same types of results might hold when considering mothers separately.

Limited Institutional Support. The studies found little interagency cooperation to assist in maintaining ties between mothers and children during and after incarceration. Zalba (1964) found a great need for coordination in developing realistic family-oriented planning and services that consider the needs of both inmate-mothers and their children, both during and following incarceration. Agency personnel should be aware of the impacts of the separation on mothers and children and the importance of normalizing expectations of inmates, children, relatives, and other relevant persons regarding visiting, letters, gifts, and financial support during and following incarceration.

With respect to prison support systems, Lundberg et al. reported institutional problems in assisting women to maintain contact with their children. The means to express grief freely and to learn to cope with the separation were minimal. Comments made by the women reflected instead pressure to suspend their emotional involvement (except for inmate relations) in order to complete the prison sentence successfully (Lundberg et al. 1975:54). There appeared to be no support for confidentiality at the prison.

Common Threads in Recommendations

Perhaps the most significant and constantly made recommendation throughout these studies is the development of intervention programs designed to maintain continuing contact between inmate-mothers and their children during the former's incarceration.

Zalba (1964) noted that the inmate-mother's own rehabilitation potential and adjustment may be affected by her maternal role and continuing relationship with her children. In the absence of clarification and stabilization of her maternal role, she may be faced with demands and crises that negatively influence her ability to complete parole following release. In this light, providing an intervention technique to retain mother-child contact during incarceration may help the child adjust to the mother's return and may provide the mother with a more realistic appraisal of her own potential to resume the maternal role.

From a slightly different standpoint, Lundberg et al. noted that prisons create a forced dependency that is "antithetical to the requirements of the mother role." Inmate-mothers become dependent upon the institution for survival and are unable to take responsibility for themselves or for their children. Therefore, it should not be surprising that they cannot resume care of their children upon release. To counter the detrimental effects of imprisonment upon mother-child relationships, the authors called for "increasing bond maintenance supports" during incarceration (Lundberg et al. 1975:59–60). Among the authors' recommendations to enhance the mother-child relationship during incarceration was the investigation of alternatives to the current system, such as nursery care within the prison or maintenance of the family in small units in the community under close supervision (ibid.:75).

Since inmate-mothers generally retained some semblence of the maternal role, Bonfanti et al. concluded that "recognition and enhancement of the maternal role in correctional policies would probably tend to promote rehabilitation as well as contribute to the family solidarity" (Bonfanti et al. 1974:117). Based on their conclusions, the authors recommended developing programs designed to prepare inmate-mothers for coping realistically with their roles as mothers following release. They suggested that these programs may be conducive to the enhancement of the mothers' self-esteem and invaluable to the adequate performance of maternal behaviors (ibid.:122). In this sense, these programs may have rehabilitative value.

Similarly, many inmate-mothers in DuBose's study expressed concern that with prolonged separation their children would develop bonds of affection more closely with caretakers than with them. In addition, the mothers noted that because the caretakers were often ill grandparents, the younger children would not be supervised adequately. They feared that by the time they were released, their children might be in trouble with the law or uncontrollable (DuBose 1975:7–8). Based on her findings, DuBose concluded that a crucial part of the rehabilitation of inmate-mothers involves successful reintegration into the family structure. She recommended providing furloughs for inmate-mothers, free transportation for their families to the prison, and conjugal visits to maintain family cohesiveness (ibid.:44). She suggested that the mechanisms to keep families intact would enhance the emotional and behavioral growth and development of members of the family unit.

Along the same line, McGowan and Blumenthal (1978) enumerated several recommendations. They urged police, judges, correctional, and parole officials to maintain greater sensitivity to a family-oriented approach regarding inmate-mothers. They suggested that a variety of programs designed to improve mother-child relationships should be developed within the institution. Program suggestions included open and extended visiting, family counseling, child-care courses, or "mother release" furloughs. They recommended closer policy and program coordination between criminal justice and social service agencies to provide more appropriate services to inmate-mothers and their children.

Related Research Efforts

In addition to research specifically dealing with inmate-mothers, other studies have included recommendations calling for closer mother-child ties during incarceration. Goodman and Price (1967) suggested provisions to allow mothers to keep their young children with them in the prison and to permit weekend visits by their older children. Eyman (1971) recommended that infants stay with their mothers in the prison. Inmates would be the primary persons responsible for the care of the children; nurseries could be established so inmate-mothers would be able to work and study. Courses in child care and homemaking could be offered as well. Wolfram (1973) recommended the encouragement of inmate-mothers to maintain ties with their families and the development of prison policies and surroundings conducive to the effort. Specific recommendations included unlimited telephone calls and mail, visits with families in residential units, and expanded use of furloughs. In a more general way, Markeley (1973) suggested that rehabilitation programs should seek to maintain and strengthen family ties. He argued that the most important factor conducive to the inmate's successful adjustment following release is strong family ties.

The recommendations made in these studies reflect assumptions which have been articulated elsewhere in the literature. Sykes (1958) noted that the most grievous aspect of imprisonment is the loss of family ties rather than the loss of liberty. Although letters, phone calls, and visits may reduce the isolation somewhat, there is the real possibility that the nature and extent of the contacts may deteriorate with the passage of time. Similarly, Goffman (1961) noted that institutions such as prisons separate persons from the larger world and from their usual status positions. In this sense, imprisoned mothers are disculturated or made incapable of engaging in aspects of their lives associated with responsibilities as mothers. This disculturation may entail significant negative psychological consequences for them such as lowering their confidence in their ability to handle their responsibilities as mothers or fearing the loss of their children's love. Their postrelease adjustment may subsequently suffer.

Summary

Previous research suggests that large proportions of incarcerated women have dependent children with whom they attempt to stay in touch during incarceration and with whom they presumably plan to live upon release. Recommendations based upon these findings usually include the development of closer ties with children during incarceration. Suggested programs range from extended visits within prisons to early release or furloughs.

One of the untested assumptions underlying these recommendations is that bond maintenance between inmate-mothers and children will positively influence mothers' self-perceptions, will reduce worries over current placement and care of children, and will better prepare them for resuming maternal responsibilities upon release. Sustained contact with children presumably will enable inmate-mothers to retain some feelings for and understanding of the family environment. Thus they may have a more realistic perspective on what to expect or demand from their children upon release.

Although not discussed previously in the literature, this involvement may entail a great deal of stress. For some women, more frequent, direct contacts with children may deepen feelings of guilt, shame, and concern for their children's welfare in their absence. For these women closer contacts may be a painful reminder of the forced separation. In addition, through such contacts some women may realize their own fears, inabilities, and perhaps lack of commitment to resume parenting responsibilities. Maintaining contact with children during imprisonment may enable mothers to determine whether or not they want to be parents upon release. Reality testing might therefore lead to conscious decisions to relinquish rather than to retain ties with children. Though unpleasant, this possibility should be borne in mind in discussing institutional programs designed to raise consciousness and facilitate bond maintenance.

Previous research has not examined existing programs to retain ties during incarceration in any detail. Therefore, the present study was undertaken with the dual objectives of expanding on previous research with an analysis of the psychological impacts of the separation from their children on inmate-mothers and describing some of the programs currently assisting inmate-mothers to retain ties with children during incarceration. The study was undertaken with the belief that a greater understanding of the impacts of the separation would generate additional questions for research and would provide practitioners with information that may be useful in considering the development of programs for bond maintenance.

Notes

1. The proportion of incarcerated children reportedly having dependent children 18 years or younger generally ranges from 56 to 68 percent. For example, in their study of homosexuality among incarcerated women in the California Institution for Women, Ward and Kassebaum (1965) reported that 68 percent of the women were mothers. Similarly, Bonfanti et al. (1974) found that 68 percent of the women in the Louisiana Correctional Institution for Women were mothers. Glick and Neto (1977) noted that 56.3 percent of their 1,607 incarcerated women in 14 states were mothers. McGowan and Blumenthal (1978) reported 67.1 percent and Baunach, in the present study, found that 66.9 percent of the imprisoned women in Kentucky and Washington state were mothers.
2. These states included California, Connecticut, Illinois, Kansas, Maine, Maryland, Massachusetts, Michigan, New Jersey, New York, North Carolina, Virginia, and West Virginia.
3. Bonfanti et al. (1974) interviewed 71 of 78 inmate-mothers in the Louisiana Correctional Institution for Women; DuBose (1975) interviewed 34 mothers at FCI-Ft. Worth; Lundberg et al. (1975) interviewed 34 of 39 inmate-mothers. From the mail survey of the McGowan and Blumenthal (1978) study, responses were received from administrators and women in 74 institutions in the United States, District of Columbia, and Puerto Rico. The published data from these respondents include information on the number and ages of children, the number of children per mother, ages of mothers, living arrangements and contacts with mothers, and future plans for reunion. In addition, interviews with 65 inmate-mothers were conducted at the New York City Correctional Institution for Women. However, none of these data were presented by the race of the mother, as will be discussed in a subsequent chapter.
4. McGowan and Blumenthal (1978) reported that about 75 percent of their national sample of inmate-mothers had been living with their dependent children prior to

arrest for the current conviction. Lundberg et al. (1975) found 74 percent and Bonfanti et al. (1974) found 66 percent.

5. McGowan and Blumenthal (1978), for instance, found that 85 percent of the inmate-mothers used the means available to stay in touch with children during incarceration. Zalba (1964), Bonfanti et al. (1974), and Lundberg et al. (1975) also found that large proportions of the inmate-mothers stayed in touch with children.

6. In Zalba's (1964) study, 34 percent of the inmate-mothers planned immediate reunions with children and another 27 percent planned reunions after a period of adjustment. Bonfanti et al. (1974) reported that nearly two-thirds of the inmate-mothers in their study planned reunions and McGowan and Blumenthal (1978) found that 78.9 percent of the inmate-mothers in their study planned to reunite with children upon release.

2

Objectives of the Study and Format of the Inquiry

Within the framework provided by previous research, the objectives of the present study were (1) to examine the effects of the separation of inmate-mothers from their children and (2) to explore programs or mechanisms designed to assist women in maintaining ties with their children in two institutions. Questions were raised regarding the nature and operations of the programs, inmates' perceptions of the programs, and the separation and its effects on them, their children, and their relationship. In this sense, the study was intended to provide a descriptive analysis of programs to generate, rather than to test, specific hypotheses and to underscore some of the major issues underlying the separation.

The Study's Objectives

Objective One: Psychological Consequences of the Separation

The first objective was to expand upon previous work in examining some of the psychological consequences of the separation of inmate-mothers from their children. The psychological consequences of the separation were divided into four general categories: perceptions of the separation; explaining mother's absence; plans for reunion; and anticipated problems in readjustment to children. Within each of these categories, several questions were raised. In addition to these psychological consequences of the separation, three other psychological aspects related to the separation were explored. These included child-rearing attitudes, inmate-mothers' self-concepts, and the impacts of involvement with drugs on mother-child relationships on the outside. The questions and issues regarding each of thse areas will be discussed briefly.

Perceptions of the Separation. Basic questions were raised about the child's care, living situation, and custody: Who cares for children during mother's incarceration? How satisfied or concerned are inmate-mothers with the care and placement of their children and why? What kinds of problems do mothers perceive that their children have encountered since their incarceration? How often do visits occur and for how long? What proportion of children were living with their mothers prior to incarceration? Have mothers been separated from children in the past because of incarceration? If so, for how long? Who has custody of the children during mother's incarceration? Were mothers forced to give up custody? If so, by whom?

Explaining Mother's Absence. Other questions concerned the extent to which mothers believed that children have a fairly realistic understanding of their absence and the events that led to it. From the mother's perspective, where do children think she is now and who told them? How do inmate-mothers explain their absence from home to their children and what reasons do they give? Where were their children at each point in the criminal justice process? Were they with their mothers at the time of the crime or at the time of arrest? Did they visit her in jail? Did they accompany her to court?

Another set of questions focused on the mothers' own reactions to the separation: What kinds of feelings do mothers in prison express about the separation (guilt, anger at themselves, bitterness at the system)? How do they handle their feelings (talk with other residents or staff, pray, get involved in activities)? Do they feel that anything in the institution will assist them in maintaining ties with or re-establishing relationships with children upon release?

Plans for Reunion and Anticipated Problems in Readjustment to Children. Planning for future reunions with children was yet another area of inquiry. What plans are being formulated by inmate-mothers regarding their children upon release? Do they plan to reunite with their children? If so, do they plan to live with children right after release or after an adjustment period? What kinds of problems, if any, do mothers think they will encounter in reestablishing relationships with their children upon release?

Child-Rearing Attitudes. An important aspect of the separation is an understanding of child-rearing attitudes among inmate-mothers. Previous research has suggested that inmate-mothers have fairly idealized perceptions of the mothering role (Bonfanti et al. 1974) and that their inability to fulfill the maternal role in prison may have some bearing on (may depress) their level of self-esteem (Lundberg et al. 1975:36). In terms of child-rearing attitudes, their isolation from dealing routinely with children and their problems may affect their ability to handle them upon release. One might, therefore, expect that inmate-mothers would favor showering their children with gifts, toys, and affection. Furthermore, given their concern and relative uncertainty about the welfare of their children, one might further expect inmate-mothers to express attitudes of protectiveness towards their children. They may, for instance, want to keep children from all possible danger and harm, perhaps to the point of unintentionally stifling creativity and development.

If, on the other hand, their imprisonment, with its requirement to constantly obey rules and regulations and conform to others' schedules, has hardened them, one might expect inmate-mothers to express attitudes reflecting punitiveness or even outright rejection of their children. For instance, punitive attitudes might be expressed through inmate-mothers' demands for instant obedience to their commands, by harsh requirements that toys be neatly arranged at all times, or through preference for the use of a great deal of physical punishment for even the slightest misbehavior. Similarly, rejecting attitudes might be expressed by regarding children as a nuisance or an inconvenience to be tolerated, preferring that children be out of the way (perhaps watching television or sleeping), and generally by questioning the value of parenthood. The general question therefore was: What are the attitudes of inmate-mothers towards raising children? Understanding these attitudes may provide an important starting point for working with inmate-mothers in parenting programs to develop a loving yet firm and consistent approach towards their children upon release.

Self-Concept. In terms of self-concept, the circumstances of their absence from children may depress the way in which inmate-mothers view themselves. Inmate-mothers, perhaps more so than other incarcerated women, may have little confidence in themselves and, particularly, in the way in which they see their relationships with family members. Whether they openly admit it or not, inmate-mothers know that the separation has been brought about by their own behavior. Thus, as the literature suggests, one might expect inmate-mothers to have an overall poor self-concept, lower than a norm group and perhaps even lower than that of other nonmothers. The questions raised along these lines included the following: How do inmate-mothers see themselves? Do they have a positive or negative view of themselves, particularly in terms of their relationships with other family members? How much confidence do they have about resuming the mothering role upon release? Is there any relationship between their child-rearing attitudes and their level of self-concept?

Two standardized instruments were used to measure child-rearing attitudes and self-concept, the Maryland Parent Attitude Survey (MPAS) and the Tennessee Self Concept Scale (TSCS). [1] The rationale for the selection of these instruments and an explanation for their use may be found in Appendix A.

Impacts of Drug Use on Mother-Child Relationships. Still another aspect of understanding the psychological consequences of the separation is a consideration of inmate-mothers who have been involved with drugs on the outside. These mothers have an added burden. Involvement with drugs may have forced them at times to behave in ways inconsistent with their desires to be a ''good'' mother. Through imprisonment, they may squarely confront themselves and the impacts on their children of their involvement with drugs. Thus, the following questions were raised about inmate-mothers' drug use: How did these women begin drug involvement? What impacts has this behavior had on their relationships with their children? How do they think their children see them and their drug involvement? What explanations did they offer their children about their behavior?

Analysis by Race of Mother. A secondary objective in understanding the psychological consequences of the separation was to analyze information by race of mother and to present any differences that were noted. None of the prior studies of inmate-mothers has included analyses of this type. However, understanding these differences may provide useful insights in meeting the needs of these women.[2] For purposes of meaningful discussion, categories of race were divided into White and Black. The latter category includes primarily Blacks but also some American Indians, Asians, and other non-White ethnic groups. All of these were combined into a single group since the proportion of non-Whites other than Blacks in the study was negligible (roughly 9 percent). In addition, statistical techniques for analyses by race included chi square tests of significance or Pearson's correlations depending upon the appropriateness of the data for the analysis (Hays 1966; Siegel 1956).

Objective Two: Program Description

Prior research has made only passing reference to currently operational programs that assist mothers and children to stay in touch with one another during incarceration. Thus, there is little information on what these programs are, what they do, and how they were started. Therefore, a second objective was to provide a descriptive analysis of programs designed to assist inmate-mothers in two prisons in maintaining ties with their children.

For purposes of this project, "program" was defined as any formal or informal mechanism that may assist a mother (1) to maintain contact with her children over and above traditional means (regular visiting hours, telephone calls, or letters); or (2) to enhance her communications skills or understanding of her own or other children.

In looking at specific programs, several questions were raised: When was the program created? Who initiated the program and why? Were residents involved in the development of the program? What obstacles, if any, were encountered in the development and implementation of the program, and how were they overcome? What is the current purpose of the program? Has the purpose changed since the program's inception? How does the program work? Are there any current problems in maintaining the program? What proportion of the resident population participates in the program at any one time? What proportion of these residents are nonmothers (if any)? How do residents perceive the program? Do nonmothers resent the intrusion of other women's children on their privacy? Or do they become involved with the children and enjoy the interaction?

In one of the sites selected for the study, Washington state, there is a unique program for women to place their children in foster care near the institution. In this site, an additional objective was to ascertain from foster parents involved in this program their perceptions of their roles and responsibilities towards children whose mothers are imprisoned. Questions included were: When and why did they decide to become involved in the program? What problems have they encountered in being foster parents for children of imprisoned mothers? Do they see their responsibilities towards children of inmate-mothers any differently from their responsibilities towards other foster children?

Format of the Inquiry

Chapter 1 anchored the inquiry within the context of research that has been conducted on the separation of inmate-mothers and children. Chapter 2 outlined the objectives of the study. The remaining chapters are divided into three areas: background characteristics and information related to objectives one and two. Chapter 3 describes background characteristics of inmate-mothers to provide the reader with an understanding of who these women are.

Chapters 4 through 6 present information related to objective one: Chapter 4 analyzes psychological consequences of the separation and describes major differences by race when they occur. Based on the data, inferences are drawn about the impacts of the separation by race of mother. Chapter 5 provides a profile of inmate-mothers' child-rearing attitudes and self-concepts and relationships between the two. Chapter 6 examines in some detail mothers' perceptions of the impact on their feelings and current relationships with their children of drug involvement prior to incarceration.

Chapters 7 and 8 provide information about objective two—program description. Chapter 7 presents an overview of the prisons studied, in looking at the programs and outlining the development and operations of the programs available at the time of the study. Since the foster care placement program in Washington state is a unique way to unite mothers and children despite the separation, Chapter 8 is devoted entirely to a description of this program and to the foster parents' perceptions of their role and responsibilities as surrogate mothers for children of imprisoned women. The book concludes with Chapter 9, which reviews principal findings and their implications and raises several questions for future examination.

Notes

1. In common parlance, the phrase self-concept is hyphenated; we have followed this practice throughout the text. However, for the formal name of the scale, Tennessee Self Concept Scale, this phrase has not been hyphenated in the text because the author of the scale has not done so. We felt it more appropriate to follow the convention used by the author in referring to his scale.
2. In fact, prior studies on inmate-mothers included too few mothers to make an analysis of background characteristics or impacts of the separation meaningful. Bonfanti et al. (1974) interviewed 71 of 78 inmate-mothers in the Louisiana Correctional Institution for Women; DuBose (1975) interviewed 34 mothers at FCI-Ft. Worth; Lundberg et al. (1975) interviewed 34 of 39 inmate-mothers. From the mail survey of the McGowan and Blumenthal (1978) study, responses were received from administrators and women in 74 institutions in the United States, District of Columbia, and Puerto Rico. The published data from these respondents includes information on the number and ages of the children, the number of children per mother, ages of mothers, living arrangements and contacts with mothers, and future plans for reunions. In addition, interviews with 65 inmate-mothers were conducted at the New York City Correctional Institution for Women. Stanton (1980) interviewed 54 mothers in California jails, children and caretakers of children in the community, and 21 mothers on probation. However, none of these data were presented by race of mothers.

3

Background Characteristics

To provide some understanding of who these inmate-mothers are, this chapter presents demographic characteristics and criminal histories for the 190 inmate-mothers incarcerated in the three prisons in Washington state and Kentucky at the time of the study.[1]

Demographic Characteristics

The following discussion is based on information given in Table 3.1.

Race, Age, and Marital Status

About half of the mothers in the three prisons were White and half were Black; however, a larger percentage of incarcerated Black women were mothers. In terms of age, most of the inmate-mothers were young. A little more than half of them (58 percent) were between the ages of 18 and 29; another 25 percent were between 30 and 35. In all, about 83 percent of the inmate-mothers were under 35 years old. However, larger proportions of Black mothers were younger and larger proportions of White mothers were older. Almost all of the White and 62 percent of the Black mothers had been married at some time in their lives. However, 38 percent of the Black and only 7 percent of the White mothers had never been married in the past. In addition, White mothers more often had been either widowed (12 percent) or divorced (45 percent).

Education, Vocational Training, and Work Experience

Both White and Black mothers had about the same level of education before prison. Approximately 69 percent of the mothers had up to eleventh-grade education. Another 27 percent had received a high school diploma or GED prior to prison, and only about 5 percent of the mothers had received any post-high school education. In addition, about 38 percent of the mothers had received any vocational training before going to prison.

TABLE 3.1
Demographic Characteristics of Inmate-Mothers, by Mother's Race

Race	White		Black		Significance[1]
	%		%		
Among all inmate-mothers	49.5	(94)	50.5	(96)	n.s.
Mothers	57	(94)	80	(96)	p= .0001
Nonmothers	43	(70)	20	(24)	
	n=	164	n=	120	
Age					
18-23	20	(20)	29	(28)	p= .0260
24-29	32	(30)	34	(33)	
30-35	22	(21)	28	(27)	
36-46	19	(18)	8	(8)	
47+	5	(5)	0	(0)	
	n=	94	n=	96	
Marital status					
Never married	7	(7)	38	(36)	
Married	25	(24)	22	(21)	p= .0001
Separated	11	(10)	15	(14)	
Widowed	12	(11)	0	(0)	
Divorced	45	(42)	25	(24)	
	n=	94	n=	95	
Education before prison					
Some college	3	(3)	6	(6)	
High school graduate/GED	28	(26)	26	(24)	n.s.
10th or 11th grade	30	(28)	39	(37)	
9th grade or less	39	(37)	29	(27)	
	n=	94	n=	94	
Vocational training before prison					
	%		%		
Yes	35	(28)	41	(28)	n.s.
No	65	(51)	59	(40)	
	n=	79	n=	68	

TABLE 3.1 *continued*

Job before prison					
Yes	54	(47)	42	(39)	n.s.
No	46	(40)	58	(53)	
		n= 87		n= 92	
Full-/part-time job					
Full time	93	(42)	63	(20)	
Part time	7	(3)	38	(12)	p= .0021
		n= 45		n= 32	
Temporary/ permanent job					
Temporary	7	(3)	31	(10)	
Permanent	93	(41)	69	(22)	
		n= 44		n= 32	
Hourly wage					
Less than $4	57	(25)	50	(17)	
$4-6	29	(13)	50	(17)	p= .05
More than $6	14	(6)	0	(0)	
		n= 44		n= 34	
Living situation before prison					
Urban	49	(45)	75	(71)	p= .0007
Rural	51	(46)	25	(24)	
		n= 91		n= 95	

1. Chi square (χ^2) tests of significance are used here. The symbol "n.s." means that χ^2 was not significant at the p < .05 level.

As with education and vocational training, there was no significant relationship between race and whether or not mothers worked before prison. Slightly less than half (48 percent) of the mothers worked before prison. Of those who worked, slightly more were White than Black. The types of jobs held by all mothers were usually those most closely associated with traditionally feminine roles (waitress, cook, secretary). For those mothers about whom information was available, more White (93 percent) than Black (63 percent) mothers worked full time and more Black (38 percent) than White (7 percent) mothers worked part time. Similarly, more White (93 percent) than Black (69 percent) mothers had permanent jobs and more Black (31 percent) than White (7 percent) mothers had temporary jobs.

Perhaps because of their job status, White mothers had earned more than Black mothers. Some White mothers earned as much as $7.50 an hour ($15,000 per year). The maximum amount earned by Black mothers was only about $6.00 an hour ($12,000 per year).

Living Situation before Prison: Urban/Rural

A significantly larger proportion of Black than White mothers were from urban as opposed to rural areas in both states. About 49 percent of the White compared with 75 percent of the Black mothers had lived in urban areas before prison. By contrast, about 51 percent of the White as compared with 25 percent of the Black mothers had lived in rural areas prior to incarceration.

Prior Criminal Record

Juvenile Record

Juvenile criminal histories were difficult to determine from institutional files. However, there was a significant correlation between race and age at first adjudication as a delinquent: As shown in Table 3.2, Black mothers had been arrested at an earlier age than White mothers. A little more than half (52 percent) of the Black compared with 28 percent of the White mothers had been arrested by age 13.[2]

Adult Record

Information about adult criminal histories was more easily obtained from institutional files. About 83 percent of the mothers had had adult arrests prior to the arrest for which they were convicted and currently incarcerated. Nearly half of these mothers were White (46 percent) and slightly more than half were Black (54 percent). In addition, Black mothers tended to have more adult arrests than White mothers. For instance, 77 percent of the Black compared with 57 percent of the White mothers had had more than four adult arrests.

About 69 percent of the mothers in the three prisons had had misdemeanor convictions in the past, and nearly half had had between one and four such convictions. With respect to age, Black mothers tended to be convicted of misdemeanors at an earlier age than White mothers. Seventy-six percent of the Black compared with 59 percent of the White mothers had had their first misdemeanor conviction by age 21. On the other hand, 32 percent of the White and only 11 percent of the Black mothers were first convicted of a misdemeanor when they were older than 25. Thus, just as when they were juveniles, adult Black mothers tended to be caught up in the criminal justice net earlier in life than White mothers. The extent to which these findings reflect discriminatory handling of Black women offenders by criminal justice authorities rather than differential impacts of environment and/or social factors is an area that bears examination in future research efforts.

Nearly half of the mothers had had prior felony convictions; of these women, most had had only one or two such convictions. As was the case

TABLE 3.2
Criminal Histories for Inmate-Mothers

Age at first adjudication delinquent	White		Black		Pearson's Correlation	Significance[1]
	%		%			
1-13	28	(7)	52	(12)	-.25	p= .040
14-19	72	(18)	48	(11)		
		n= 25		n= 23		

Number of prior adult arrests						
1-3	43	(31)	23	(20)		
4-9	34	(25)	38	(32)	.21	p= .003
10+	23	(17)	39	(33)		
		n= 73		n= 85		

Number of misdemeanor convictions						
1-4	75	(45)	63	(45)		
5+	25	(15)	37	(26)	.11	n.s.
		n= 60		n= 71		

Age at first misdemeanor conviction						
1-18	25	(14)	40	(29)		
19-21	34	(19)	36	(26)		
22-24	9	(5)	13	(9)	-.24	p= .003
25+	32	(18)	11	(8)		
		n= 56		n= 72		

Number of prior felony convictions						
1	66	(27)	57	(30)		
2	17	(7)	17	(9)		
3+	17	(7)	26	(14)	.11	n.s.
		n= 41		n= 53		

Age at first felony conviction						
	%		%			
1-18	8	(3)	14	(7)		
19-21	23	(9)	36	(19)		
22-24	23	(9)	23	(12)	-.21	p= .022
25+	46	(18)	27	(14)		
		n= 39		n= 52		

1. Chi square (χ^2) tests of significance are used here. The symbol "n.s." means that χ^2 was not significant at the $p < .05$ level.

with misdemeanors, race was unrelated to the number of prior felony convictions. However, as with prior misdemeanors, Black mothers tended to be convicted of their first felony at an earlier age than White mothers. More specifically, about half of the Black and 69 percent of the White mothers were convicted of their first felony when they were older than 22, whereas about half of the Black and only about 31 percent of the White mothers were convicted of their first felony before age 22.

Family Criminal Record

There is some concern for the problem of transmission of criminal behavior from one generation to another. Stanton (1980), for instance, reported that 44 percent of her 54 jail mothers had parents and siblings in jail and another 9 percent had only a parent in jail (Stanton 1980:4). In our study, for 53 percent of the imprisoned mothers on whom data were obtained, other family members had criminal records. Unlike in Stanton's study, these other family members were primarily siblings (59 percent), husbands, ex-husbands, or lovers (28 percent), and, to a lesser extent, children (7 percent) or at least one parent (5 percent). Interestingly, whether or not the woman's family had a criminal record was significantly related to race: larger proportions of Black (65 percent) compared with White (41 percent) mothers had other family members with a criminal record. Moreover, more Black (71 percent) than White (40 percent) mothers had siblings with criminal records (See Table 3.3).

There has been some interest in whether or not women are becoming more involved in committing crimes on their own as opposed to simply serving as an accomplice with someone else, usually a man. If indeed women are becoming more independent, so the argument goes, then they may be engaging in crimes on their own more frequently. Although information in the present study does not consider changes in trends over time and includes only inmate-mothers, it is possible to gain some insights on this question. As Table 3.3 shows, more than half of the mothers on whom data were obtained (58 percent) committed the crime alone for the current conviction. Another 23 percent committed the crime with one man. For the 78 mothers who committed the crime with others, a majority of them had served as an accomplice (58 percent) or partner (36 percent) and only a few (6 percent) had perpetrated the crime, that is, served as leaders.

Offenses of Conviction

Table 3.4 reports the proportions of respondents convicted of various offenses. This information takes account of the fact that women offenders may be convicted of and serving time on more than one offense providing a more accurate picture of offenses for which women are incarcerated than is common.[3] About half of the mothers had been convicted of property offenses and

TABLE 3.3
Criminal Record for Other Family Members

Family criminal record	White		Black		Significance[1]
	%		%		
Yes	41	(36)	65	(60)	p= .002
No	59	(51)	35	(33)	
		n= 87		n= 93	
Who has record					
Siblings	40	(15)	71	(42)	
Husband/lover/ ex-husband	38	(14)	22	(13)	p= .05
Children	11	(4)	5	(3)	
Parents	11	(4)	2	(1)	
		n= 37		n= 59	
Commit crime alone					
Alone	53	(48)	63	(59)	
With 1 Man	29	(26)	17	(16)	n.s.
With 1 Woman	8	(7)	11	(10)	
With 1 Man/Woman	10	(9)	9	(8)	
		n= 90		n= 93	
Perpetrator/ accomplice/ partners					
Perpetrator	4	(2)	9	(3)	n.s.
Accomplice	64	(28)	50	(17)	
Partners	32	(14)	41	(14)	
		n= 44		n= 34	

1. Chi square (χ^2) tests of significance are used here. The symbol "n.s." means that χ^2 was not significant at the p < .05 level.

a little more than a third had been convicted of person offenses. With respect to drug offenses, nearly one-fourth of the mothers had been convicted of buying/selling and possession/use. The two single offenses for which the largest proportion of mothers had been convicted were forgery (20 percent) and larceny/theft (17 percent). The only offenses significantly related to race were drug offenses. For both buying/selling and possession/use, there were small but significant correlations with race: Black mothers were more often convicted of these drug offenses than White mothers.

Number of Children

The mothers interviewed had a total of 300 children or an average of 2.2 children each. About 84 percent of the mothers had 3 children or less. Only

TABLE 3.4
Proportion of Mothers Convicted of Each Type of Offense, by Race[1]

Property offenses	White		Black		Total	
	%		%		%	
Larceny-theft	14	(13)	20	(19)	17	(32)
Forgery	23	(22)	17	(16)	20	(38)
Stolen property	9	(8)	5	(5)	7	(13)
Burglary	6	(6)	4	(4)	5	(10)
Arson	3	(3)	1	(1)	2	(4)
Total	55	(52)	47	(45)	51	(97)
Person offenses						
Robbery	12	(11)	13	(12)	12	(23)
Murder	8	(8)	6	(6)	7	(14)
Manslaughter	10	(9)	10	(10)	10	(19)
Assault	7	(7)	6	(6)	7	(13)
Total	37	(35)	35	(34)	36	(69)
Drug offenses						
Buying/selling	10	(9)	19	(18)	14	(27)[2]
Possession/use	5	(5)	14	(14)	10	(19)[3]
Total	15	(14)	33	(32)	24	(46)
Other						
Escape	4	(4)	1	(1)	3	(5)
Miscellaneous (kidnapping; unlawful imprisonment; motor vehicle theft; sexual offenses)	11	(10)	6	(6)	8	(16)
Total	15	(14)	7	(7)	11	(21)
		n= 94		n= 96		n= 190

1. Percentages exceed 100 percent because mothers may have been convicted of more than one offense.
2. Relationship between conviction for Buying/selling drugs and Race: $r = -.15$, $p = .02$.
3. Relationship between conviction for Possession/use of drugs and Race: $r = -.13$, $p = .03$.

4 (3 percent) mothers interviewed had 6 children and 1 (1 percent) had 7 children. Data for 283 of the 300 children were obtained. This includes data for each of the 4 youngest children. The average ages of the 4 youngest children were 6.7 years, 9.0 years, 10.5, years and 11.8 years. Approximately two-thirds of the children were under age 10 and thus separated from their mothers relatively early in life. Race and number of children were not significantly related. Mothers had been separated from children for an average of about 18 months.

Summary

These data present a profile for White and Black mothers. A higher percentage of Black than White inmates are mothers. Black mothers tend to be younger, less frequently married, and more often from urban areas prior to incarceration than White mothers. Both White and Black mothers have equally poor educations, little vocational training prior to entering prison, and only some work experience. Both groups usually have held traditionally "female" jobs, but White mothers generally have had permanent, full-time jobs, whereas Black mothers have had temporary, part-time jobs. With respect to prior criminal record, though juvenile records were difficult to trace, data indicate that Black mothers had first been involved with the juvenile authorities at an earlier age than White mothers. Similarly, with respect to adult prior records, Black mothers had come into contact with the adult criminal justice system earlier in life than White mothers for both misdemeanor and felony offenses. In addition, current convictions reflect more drug offenses for Black than for White mothers.

These characteristics of inmate-mothers provide a backdrop against which the psychological consequences of the separation may be examined, particularly the variations in the impacts of the separation by race of mother.

Notes

1. The entire study included demographic characteristics and criminal history information on all of the 284 women incarcerated in the two women's prisons in Kentucky and one in Washington state. In addition, extensive interviews with 196 (69 percent) volunteers were conducted. Of these 196 women, 138 (70 percent) were mothers of children 18 years old or younger and 58 (30 percent) were nonmothers. Statistical analyses of background characteristics and criminal histories indicated that there were no significant differences between the women interviewed and those not interviewed. The selected sample thus reflects a random sample of the population under study. Therefore, background information for all 190 mothers imprisoned in the three prisons is presented. In addition, it must be noted that of the 284 women in the three prisons, 190 (66.9 percent) were mothers and 94 (33.1 percent) were nonmothers. Therefore, the sample of 138 mothers interviewed included 72.6 percent of all mothers imprisoned in two states. To my knowledge, this is the largest sample of inmate-mothers interviewed in depth in any study of this nature to date. Given the size of the sample, conclusions may be comfortably generalized to the populations under study.

2. Information on juvenile records was frequently not included in institutional files for adults. The information presented here on age at first adjudication delinquent is mainly suggestive given the small sample size (n = 48).

3. Sixty mothers (32 percent, n = 190) were serving time for multiple crimes: 55 percent of these mothers were White and 45 percent were Black. There was no significant relationship between race and whether or not mothers were serving time on multiple crimes.

4

Impacts of the Separation, by Mother's Race

The psychological consequences of the separation for inmate-mothers include many complex and confused feelings. Overall, women of all backgrounds expressed despondency and guilt that their own behavior had created the situation. However, White and Black mothers showed some distinct patterns in their responses to the separation. This chapter delineates these responses and their implications for understanding the separation.

Perceptions of the Separation

Current Caretakers

The question who is caring for children is one of the primary concerns of inmate-mothers. Mothers in prison often remarked that they could "do time" somewhat easier knowing that their children were placed with someone they trusted. Nearly all (82 percent) of the 283 children were in the care of family members. About 36 percent were living with their mother's parents, most often with her mother. Another 25 percent of the children were living with other relatives such as aunts, uncles, or siblings, and an additional 20 percent were living with the child's natural father. Less frequently, children were placed with nonrelatives such as friends or in foster homes or were on their own.

As for the relationship between race and current caretakers, significantly more Black than White children were living with the woman's parents, and more White than Black children lived with the child's father or nonrelatives (Table 4.1). These findings suggest that an inmate-mother's family, primarily her own parents, provide the major source of caretakers for her children. Furthermore, when the mother's ethnic background is taken into account, significantly different patterns of child placement are evident. Among Black mothers, particularly, parents tend to care for children during incarceration. White mothers, however, may not have parents who are available or willing to care for children.

TABLE 4.1
Current Caretakers and Mother's Satisfaction
with Placement of Children

	White		Black		Significance[1]
Caretaker	%		%		
Parents	23	(34)	51	(68)	
Other Relatives	23	(34)	29	(38)	$p < .001$
Natural Father	29	(44)	10	(13)	
Nonrelatives	25	(39)	10	(13)	
	n= 151^2		n= 132^2		
Satisfaction					
Very satisfied	45	(68)	61	(80)	
Satisfied	31	(46)	26	(35)	$p < .05$
Dissatisfied	13	(20)	10	(13)	
Very dissatisfied	11	(16)	3	(4)	
	n= 150^2		n= 132^2		

1. Chi square (χ^2) tests of significance are used here.
2. The sample size here refers to the number of children.

Satisfaction with Placement

For 81 percent of the children, mothers were generally satisfied with the current placement. Most of these women had placed their children with relatives and had had some role in deciding where the placement would be. The remaining mothers were generally dissatisfied with their children's living situation. Moreover, mothers of Black children tended to be more satisfied with placements than mothers of White children (Table 4.1).

Dissatisfaction was frequently expressed by mothers who had little say in placing their children, by mothers with children in different placements, especially with strangers, or, often by White mothers whose children were placed with nonrelatives. Many mothers felt it would be hard on young children in a strange environment to have little contact with siblings. However, when the placements were with different relatives, mothers expressed more satisfaction mainly because they felt more comfortable knowing something about the caretaker's background and concern for the child's welfare. In addition, many mothers said their children would be able to see one another or visit them in prison more easily if living with relatives.

A small number of mothers expressed concern even though children were placed with relatives. One Black mother, for example, whose three children were placed with her older daughter, said their clothes were not clean, their hair was unkempt, and they "looked unpresentable" to go to school. Other White mothers expressed dissatisfaction because they felt the caretakers, especially nonrelatives, were trying to take the children away and, as one mother put it, "to raise them up to be somebody I don't even know."

Children's Problems

Each mother was asked to indicate whether or not each of her children had had any problems since her incarceration. If the child had had any, she was asked to indicate what types of problems had been encountered.

With respect to the first question, for about half of the children, mothers reported that the children either did not have any problems (38 percent), or that they were unaware of any problems (13 percent). There was no significant relationship between race and whether mothers thought that the children had developed any problems since their incarceration. That for nearly half of the children mothers were unaware of any problems suggests one of two possibilities. On one hand, children may in fact not have run into any difficulties since their mother's incarceration, and their mothers have an accurate understanding of their welfare. On the other hand, it may be that mothers do not have enough contact with their children or the caretakers to be fully aware of the problems their children experience during their absence.

Regardless of race, mothers felt that their children had developed only one or two problems since their incarceration. The problems mothers cited fall into three groups: physical, emotional or psychological, and academic. Problems placed in one of these groups may, of course, be related to problems in another. For example, poor school work or health problems may be a function of underlying emotional upset. However, since mothers identified academic and medical problems separately, they are discussed in this manner.

By far the largest proportion of problems (70 percent) reported were psychological or emotional. These problems were mainly restlessness, or "hypertension" as the mothers called it, aggressive behavior, or withdrawal. With respect to "hypertension," mothers indicated that their children fussed, paced the floor, or cried more often since their incarceration and frequently asked them or caretakers when they were coming home.

Aggressive behavior was more frequently reported for younger children. Mothers noted that these children often reacted hostilely towards caretakers, especially nonrelatives. In discussing their children's aggressive behavior, many mothers expressed concern that, without proper guidance, their children might get involved in crime as they got older. In fact, a few mothers noted that their older children had already been arrested for petty offenses.

A few mothers who said that their children had withdrawn noted that they had experienced the children's withdrawal from themselves during visiting. In these cases, the children reportedly sat quietly or paid more attention to the person who brought them. These mothers were alarmed that their children were pulling away from them. More frequently, mothers said that their children were withdrawing from those around them at home and had not been like that before their incarceration. These mothers were concerned about their children's ability to relate to others as they grew up.

About 15 percent of the problems mothers reported were academic, mostly poor school work. Mothers who mentioned these problems were concerned that their children might not be receiving an education that would benefit them later in life. The other problems noted were physical. Many mothers worried that their children, especially those with known medical deficiencies, might not be getting proper medical attention in their absence.

Visits with Children

The most direct way to retain ties with children during incarceration is through visits. However, slightly less than half (47 percent) of the children visited their mothers regularly, once a month or more. The most frequently given reasons for few visits were the distance from the children's placement or the lack of transportation. The frequency of visits was not significantly related to race; that is, regardless of race, the problems inherent in getting the children to prisons far from home are important determinants of the extent to which inmate-mothers and children visit one another.

Children's Living Situation prior to Mother's Incarceration

Incarcerated mothers may express concern for their children mainly because the prison environment is highly conducive to doing so, but, unless she had lived with her children prior to her incarceration, her expressed concern would seem unfounded and hollow. Therefore, it was important to determine whether or not mothers had lived with their children prior to incarceration and how often other separations had occurred in the past.

Nearly three-fourths of the children had been living with their natural mothers before incarceration. This was true for a significantly larger proportion of Black than of White children. Children not living with their natural mother prior to her incarceration had been living with their natural father, with her parents, with other relatives, primarily in-laws, or with nonrelatives. Among these children, more Black than White children had lived with the inmate-mother's parents or with relatives other than the natural father. Similarly, more White children had lived with their natural fathers or with nonrelatives (Table 4.2).

Regardless of age, about 62 percent of the children had not been separated from their mothers in the past because of incarceration. Additional evidence to support minimal separations in the past comes from prior record information. Only 46 or about 24 percent of the 190 mothers had served as long as six months in state prisons in the past. Roughly 81 percent of the White and 71 percent of the Black mothers had not been separated in the past because

TABLE 4.2
Children's Living Situation prior to Mother's Incarceration

Children who lived with natural mother or others:	White		Black		Significance[1]
	%		%		
Natural mother	67	(99)	82	(107)	
All others combined	33	(48)	18	(23)	p < .005
		n= 147		n= 130	
Children who lived with others:					
Natural father	44	(21)	22	(5)	
Woman's parents	19	(9)	39	(9)	p < .005
Other relatives	8	(4)	30	(7)	
Nonrelatives	29	(14)	9	(2)	
		n= 48		n= 23	

1. Chi square (χ^2) tests of significance are used here

of incarceration. Although the accuracy of records information about prior incarceration may be questionable, these findings generally suggest that up until the mother's current incarceration, most of the children had been living with their mothers on a continuous basis and that this incarceration was the first major change for them.[1]

Legal Custody of Children

Whether or not inmate-mothers indicated that they retained custody of their children depended on the nature of the question asked. Two questions were raised: Who has custody of your children now? and Were you forced to give up custody of your children? The response to the first question indicated that about 43 percent of the children were in custody of their inmate-mother at the time of the study. Children of Black mothers were more often still in the custody of their parents than children of White mothers, although higher proportions of White than Black children were in the custody of other relatives, nonrelatives, or the children's natural father (see Table 4.3).

When mothers were asked the second question, whether or not they were forced to relinquish custody, a slightly different set of responses was obtained. For 24 of the children, mothers who had said in response to the previous question that their own mothers temporarily had custody of their children, responded now that they had not in fact given up custody but that they themselves retained custody even though their mothers were caring for the children. Thus, responses to this question indicated that inmate-mothers still had custody of about 51 percent (or 144) of the children, 41 percent (or 59) White and 59 percent (or 85) Black children.[2] For 39 percent of the 118

TABLE 4.3
Legal Custody of Children

Current custodian	White		Black		Significance[1]
	%		%		
Natural mother	32	(48)	56	(72)	
Woman's parents	12	(19)	22	(28)	
Natural father	16	(24)	5	(6)	p < .001
Other relatives	20	(29)	12	(16)	
Nonrelatives	20	(29)	5	(6)	
		n= 149		n= 128	
Was mother forced to relinquish custody?					
Yes	49	(38)	20	(8)	
No, but she did give up custody	51	(39)	80	(33)	p < .005
		n= 77		n= 41	

1. Chi square (χ^2) tests of significance are used here.

children for whom mothers reported that they had given up custody, mothers said they had been forced to do so, whereas for 61 percent of these children, mothers said they had done so voluntarily. Considering these data in terms of race, the custody for more White than Black children had been given up forcibly, whereas for more Black than White children custody had been relinquished at the mother's discretion (Table 4.3).

Explaining Mother's Absence

When mothers go to prison they may or may not have a chance, or want, to discuss the circumstances of their absence with the children. The extent and nature of contacts from the time of the offense to the arrival in prison depends upon circumstances beyond the mother's control. Yet, an important question is whether, given the opportunity, mothers do tell those children who are able to understand what is happening. Despite the unfavorable circumstances surrounding the separation, do mothers want children to understand that they have done something wrong?

Perceptions of Where Mother Is

Most of the mothers, regardless of race, wanted their children to know the truth about the separation. About 68 percent said that their children knew they were in prison or, as some women said, "jail or a place to be punished." Less than 10 percent said their children believed they were away at school or college, at work, in a hospital, or visiting relatives. An additional 21 percent said that they did not know where their children thought they were. Following arrest, some mothers said they never had a chance to tell the children and were not sure what information had been provided by caretakers about their absence. Two other mothers said their children had definite but inaccurate ideas about their absence. One mother said that her only young son thought the institution was her home. He had been born since she came to the prison and had visited her there once a week. For him, prison was "where mothers are supposed to live." Another mother said that her two ex-husbands had told her two children that she was dead. Consequently, her attempts to write letters to the children were futile.

Who Told Children

About 51 percent of the mothers told their children "where they are now." Most of them had explained at the time of arrest or at some time prior to imprisonment that they were going away to be punished. Some mothers, however, said that they had found it difficult initially to accept their incarceration and thus were unable to tell their children. Often, these mothers waited until children raised questions after incarceration to explain their absence. A few mothers commented that, in the interim, well-meaning relatives had told the children that they were visiting friends or working. Angered at this deception, some of the mothers told the children the truth. One mother noted, "My mother told her I was away on vacation . . . because [my daughter] is so young. When I found that out I got mad. I wanted her to know the truth so I told her myself." Another mother commented that she did not have a chance to talk with her children about her absence until she reached the prison. However, the first time she saw them in prison she explained why she was not with them:

> My mother explained to them . . . that I was in a hospital. Once I was here, I was able to explain to my oldest son that I was never in a hospital. At one time she even went so far as to say that I was too busy and that I couldn't see them. I just went off. I mean don't tell my kids that I am too busy. If I was still a child and they were to tell me that, I wouldn't like it. I told them that I wasn't in a hospital and that I had done something wrong and had to be here for a while.

Other mothers (18 percent), primarily White, said that other relatives (13 percent) or nonrelatives (5 percent) had explained the absence and that they concurred. Since these women often had not seen their children following arrest, they had not had an opportunity to discuss the situation with them. Consequently, when caretakers provided an explanation, mothers went along with it whether or not it was true. About 12 percent of the mothers said their children learned the truth on their own. Some children had been at the scene of the crime, at the arrest, or had visited mother in jail and knew that she would have to be away, although the reasons may have been unclear. Other older children had read about the crime in the newspapers or had heard their mother's name mentioned in conjunction with a crime during news broadcasts.

The other mothers (18 percent) said they did not know who explained their absence to the children. They thought that caretakers probably had told children that they would be gone but were unsure what details had been conveyed. These mothers expressed the most concern as they feared children would have erroneous impressions or would not understand the situation. Many of these mothers commented that they wanted the chance to discuss their absence with the children directly.

Among these mothers who knew how children had learned of their whereabouts, Black more frequently than White mothers had told children where they were themselves (Table 4.4).

Explanations for the Absence

Mothers were asked to provide a rationale as to why they had explained their absence to their children as they did. Some mothers gave two or more reasons for their explanations. Overall there was no significant relationship between the types of reasons given and the race of the mother. About 54 percent of the mothers said that given the opportunity they told their children that they were going to be punished for bad behavior; they wanted their children to know at the outset why they were leaving. One White mother said, "Why lie? They'll find out sooner or later from somebody and I'd rather it be from me than the neighbor's kids or some stranger." Some mothers feared that children would otherwise learn the truth elsewhere and might lose respect for them. This was particularly true of Black mothers. Black more often than White mothers said they wanted to make sure children learned the truth from them rather than from somebody else (Table 4.5).

Another 38 percent of the mothers said their children were capable of understanding the real reason for their absence, and about one-third said the

TABLE 4.4
Who Told Children Where Mother Is[1]

	White		Black		Significance[2]
	%		%		
Natural mother	52	(30)	74	(41)	
Relatives	17	(10)	15	(8)	
Nonrelatives	12	(7)			p= .02
Children found out themselves	19	(11)	11	(6)	
		n= 58		n= 55	

1. Data on race for the 25 mothers who did not know who told children of their absence was not obtained and therefore not included in the table.
2. Chi square (χ^2) tests of significance are used here.

TABLE 4.5
Mothers' Reasons to Explain Her Absence

Reason	Number	Percentage of Mothers Reporting This Reason[1]	Percentage of Reasons[2]
Tell child the truth[3]	75	54	34
Child capable of understanding	52	38	23
Child should know where mother is	44	32	20
Child too young to understand	34	25	15
Child may be affected negatively	11	8	5
Never saw child to explain	7	5	3
Total	223		100

1. Total percentage exceeds 100.0 percent because some mothers gave more than one reason to explain their absence. The denominator for these percentages in this column is 138, the number of mothers interviewed.
2. The denominator for the percentages in this column is 223, the total number of reasons given. Percentages do not equal 100 percent because of rounding error.
3. This category includes the significant relationship between Race and if the reason was given, as follows:

   Never lie to children:
   White 23 (36 percent), Black 34 (59 percent), Significance p = .02. Chi square (χ^2) test of significance is used here.

children had a right to know the truth. About a quarter, usually those with children under age 2, said the children were too young to understand why they were away. Many of them often added that they planned to explain what had happened when the children grew up. Still other mothers (8 percent) felt that children might be hurt more if they knew mother was in prison. A frequent comment was that, "They don't need to know. They've gone through enough already with me just being away. Someday I'll probably tell them all about it." Some argued that children might worry about their mother's care given stereotyped beliefs about jail derived from television or movies. Other mothers admitted that they did not know how to explain their incarceration.

Mothers' Feelings about the Separation

Many mothers were ashamed and embarrassed that their behavior had led to imprisonment and separation and feared that their children would think they were unloved, or as one woman put it, "that I did something because I wanted to leave." Explaining their absence to children entailed both providing a justification for the criminal behavior and assuring children that they had not intended this behavior to lead to the separation. Mothers often said that these two conflicting points were difficult to convey to children who realized most clearly that "mommie is gone."

These data generally suggest that mothers honestly want to tell their children that they have done something bad and have gone away as a punishment.[3] Moreover, they prefer to tell the children themselves. Yet, some mothers find it difficult to be truthful because they do not want to be rejected or to hurt their children further. Women with older children frequently remarked that they wanted their own incarceration to serve as an indication of what children could expect if they break the law.

The most common feelings expressed by inmate-mothers were guilt and despondency. Regardless of the nature of the crime, their own behavior had resulted in the separation from children. The burden of what was happening both to them and to their children was thus weighing heavily on their shoulders. Mothers convicted of property crimes were in a double bind. They were ashamed and angry at themselves for their involvement in the crime, but added that they had no alternative means to obtain what they needed, even if it was money for drugs. Yet, these women often said that they might have acted differently had they realized the potential consequences of their behavior. Mothers convicted of offenses against persons, however, said that the incident had happened so fast that it had been unavoidable. Reconciling that they had been convicted of a crime and separated from their children with their expressed love and concern for their children created a great deal of stress and despair that remained unabated for many mothers in the sterile prison environment.

In handling their feelings most mothers, regardless of race, preferred to be alone and write letters or pray. Many others said that they liked to get involved in activities in the prison so they would have less time to dwell on the separation. Some liked to talk about their feelings with other residents. Very few women preferred talking with staff mainly because they feared negative reprisals, such as bad write-ups or being placed in the cellblock.

Where Children Were at the Time of the Offense

About one-third of the mothers (34 percent) on whom data were obtained said that their children were with them at the time of the offense. Many of these children were of preschool age. Other mothers (13 percent) mostly Black, said that their children were with their own mothers. The remaining mothers (53 percent) said that their children were with someone else (another relative, friend, babysitter, foster home). These results occurred with about equal frequency for White and Black mothers (Table 4.6).

Mothers convicted of crimes against persons (murder, manslaughter, assault) said more frequently that their children were with them at the time of

TABLE 4.6
Children's Presence at Time of Offense, Arrest, Court, and Jail Visits

	White		Black[1]		Significance[2]
	%		%		
At offense child with:[3]					
Mother	38	(16)	29	(10)	
Woman's mother	5	(2)	24	(8)	n.s.
Other (relatives, friends, baby sitter, etc.)	26	(11)	24	(8)	
Not sure	31	(13)	24	(8)	
		n= 42		n= 34	
At arrest child with:[3]					
Mother	38	(16)	28	(10)	n.s.
Woman's mother	12	(5)	30	(11)	
Other (relatives, friends, baby sitter, etc.)	50	(21)	42	(15)	
		n= 42		n= 36	
Was child in court?[3]					
Yes	33	(13)	29	(8)	n.s.
No	67	(26)	71	(20)	
		n= 39		n= 28	
Did child visit mom in jail?[3]					
Yes	39	(17)	47	(14)	n.s.
No	61	(27)	53	(16)	
		n= 44		n= 30	

1. Percentages exceed 100 percent because of rounding error.
2. Chi square (χ^2) tests of significance are used here. The symbol "n.s." means that χ^2 was not significant at the $p < .05$ level.
3. These questions were added to the interview after the data collection began. Therefore, information was not obtained for all mothers interviewed.

the incident. Often these incidents occurred very quickly in or near the woman's home. Although they admitted that they would have preferred that their children had not been there, they could not change the circumstances. As one mother said:

> It all happened so fast. He was there with me when I fired the gun. I didn't want it that way. But it couldn't be helped.

Another inmate-mother who had been arrested for assault said:

> Two women came in and jumped me in my own house. I was cooking dinner. I had a knife in my hand when I opened the door. Next thing I knew, I was attacked and being beaten from here to kingdom come. One woman fell off of me onto the floor. My daughter was terrified at seeing her mommie hurt.

Another woman convicted of murder said:

> The man I killed—he was a trick. He came to my house and the kids were in bed. He gave me $100. I slammed the door in his face. He broke the glass on the door and came in. I told him to keep the kids from waking. I gave him back his money. He didn't take the money but was still raising hell. I thought he was tripping out on acid or something.
>
> My kids were hollering, "Mama, Mama"; they came running around my legs saying they were hungry. I told him to leave because I had to feed my kids and take them out for a walk. He was hollering that he wasn't going no damn where so I said, "Oh, yeah?"
>
> He took one of my twin boys and threw him up to the ceiling and just stepped back and my son hit the concrete floor and he laid there. He was unconscious. I thought he was dead. I got mad and we started fighting. I kept a knife behind the couch and just stabbed him.

Often, inmate-mothers whose children were at the scene of the incident said that they could not help what happened but that they were shocked that they could commit such a violent act in front of their children. One inmate-mother serving a 20-year sentence on manslaughter summed it up this way:

> There was a lot of tension. Well, I shot this lady. Then I just blacked out. If I hadn't turned around and seen my [1-year-old] son, I probably would have done a lot more damage. I saw him and it made me come to my senses. I realized that I didn't want to do this in front of him. But when you get mad, your nerves play funny tricks on you and you don't see nothing except that you don't like this person.

For women involved in property crimes (grand larceny, forgery, embezzlement, arson, burglary), the children were usually not with them at the time of the incident. They were still at home, in school, or visiting relatives or friends. To some extent, property crimes involve a certain amount of preparation beforehand, so mothers tended to make sure that their children were not around when the incident occurred. In addition, property crimes are most often committed outside the home and therefore away from children. For instance, one 25-year-old Black mother said, "Even though I lived with my husband, I wasn't able to support the kids without stealing. So I would go out and take things while they were in school." A White woman convicted of forgery said that she "wrote bad checks to keep me and my kids going. They were with me all the time—we lived out of the back of my car—but they were too young to know what was going on."

Where Children Were at the Time of Arrest

For nearly half of the mothers (46 percent) on whom data were obtained, the children were not with them or the grandmothers at the time of arrest. They were often with friends, a babysitter, visiting relatives, or living in a foster home. For about one-third of the mothers, the children were with them, and for other mothers (21 percent), with their own mothers at the time of arrest (Table 4.6).

There seemed to be no consistent pattern in terms of where the children were at the time their mothers were arrested for various types of crimes. For crimes against persons, even if the children had been present when the incident occurred, the mothers may have called a neighbor, relative, or friend to come get them as soon as possible. Often, they arrived right after the police. For instance, one inmate-mother convicted of manslaughter said that her mother arrived just as she was being taken downtown:

> As soon as I called the rescue squad, I called my mother. My mother and brother came to the house. My mother got there just as the police got through questioning my little sister. I was being taken downtown. My daughter went with her.

Sometimes the mothers were not picked up right after the incident and were arrested when their children were at school or at home. One inmate-mother convicted of murder was arrested at her sister's house several days later:

> Two of my three children were with me when I was arrested. The third was in school. We were living at my sister's house when they arrested me and my sister said, "You have got to be kidding."

Similarly, mothers convicted of property crimes may have been arrested while children were with them, with other friends or relatives, or in school. If their children were away from home, mothers sometimes had a chance to arrange for someone to meet them when they returned. Mothers who had no such chance usually said they were upset and concerned that their children would not know what happened.

The finding that there is no consistent pattern of children's whereabouts when mothers were arrested for various types of crimes is not surprising, since people generally have no control over where or when they will be arrested. Yet, these findings are in sharp contrast to the common assumption that mothers are whisked away in the dead of night leaving small children alone to fend for themselves. Although this pattern did occur in some cases in the present study, it was more the exception than the rule. For those cases in which the children were with their mothers at the time of arrest, most mothers said that there was someone else there to take care of the children or that they had an opportunity to call someone before they were taken into custody or when they got to jail.

Whether or not mothers had a chance to explain what happened and why they were leaving before they were arrested and taken away seemed to depend more upon the arresting police officer's attitudes and cooperation than upon anything else. Some women said that police let them take the time to talk briefly with their children, others noted that they were not given the time. For instance, one mother serving time on manslaughter and assault said:

> They carried my child past the dead body. There was no call for that. She didn't do it. . . . I didn't get a chance to talk to my children. The cops did and I have no knowledge of what the cops said to my kids. I have no idea what they said. My husband was there but he went into a big shock. The kids were really there with the cops.

Another woman arrested for a drug charge said that she was at least allowed to take her 3-year-old son with her to the police station and to arrange for someone to come pick him up:

> He didn't understand what was going on. He just saw people kicking me around and tearing up our house. All I could do was hold him and tell him everything was going to be OK. He started crying. They let me take him to the jail with me and I called my sister and told her to come and pick him up. I told him I was going to be away awhile and that I would be with him as soon as possible.

Children in Court with Mother

About two-thirds (69 percent) of the mothers on whom data were obtained said that their children did not appear in court with them; the remaining mothers (31 percent) said that their children did go to court with them (Table 4.6). The most common reasons for not having the children there were: that they were too young, that court was no place for children, that they were in school, and, most importantly, that the mothers did not want them there. Mothers were generally afraid that their children would see them collapse under the strain of the courtroom proceedings. One inmate-mother convicted of embezzlement put it rather forcefully:

> No! I didn't want her there! I didn't want her to hear the things they were saying about me and see me fall apart—which I did.

Often, mothers who said that children accompanied them to court had no other place to leave them. This was primarily true for mothers with very young children, who had been out on bond or on personal recognizance and who had no other relatives or friends nearby. Sometimes, however, mothers said that their children were required to appear in court:

> I'm here on a manslaughter charge. I was out on bond. . . . My [11-year-old] son knew everything. He had to be there to get up in court and tell the last time he had seen [the man I killed]. I think it kind of made him nervous. . . . He understood what happened because he had seen [the man] beat me a lot. And he really got to know that I would probably be gone. I explained to him that I would have to go away for a while.

Children's Visits with Mother in Jail

A little more than half (58 percent) of the mothers on whom data were obtained said that their children did not visit them in jail; the others (42 percent) said that their children did visit them in jail (Table 4.6). Some mothers said their children were not allowed to visit because they were under 18. Many did not want their children to come to the jail because the visiting conditions were so oppressive. Often county jails had only telephones and glass windows through which brief visits might be conducted. Very rarely were the women allowed to have any physical contact with visitors. Under these circumstances, mothers preferred not to see children at all. One mother said:

> We had a good relationship up until then. I didn't want to have to talk to my kids through a phone and glass window. I couldn't even touch them. What would they have thought about it or about me? It might have scared them half to death to see me like that.

Mothers, therefore, usually waited until they got into a prison where visiting conditions were more relaxed. At least there they could sit with their children and talk in more favorable circumstances. Other mothers simply had not accepted their own plight and emotionally could not handle seeing children just yet. One mother remarked:

> It was hard on both of us. I couldn't believe that I was in jail. I didn't want to believe it and I didn't want to put them through seeing me like that. So I didn't have any visits with my kids until I got to [the prison].

Mothers who preferred to have visits with children in jail, despite the circumstances, were often afraid that they would be unable to see their children in prison because of the distance from their homes. Thus, they wanted to take advantage of every available opportunity to see their children before they were taken far away from them.

These data indicate that the circumstances surrounding the initial separation of inmate-mothers and their children were varied. Some mothers simply left for a few hours to be booked and returned home on personal recognizance or bond. These women had the chance to discuss the events with their children and to prepare them for possible separation in the near future. Most other mothers were taken away and placed in jail. The nature and extent of subsequent contacts with their children depended upon circumstances beyond their control.

Many mothers who did not have a chance to explain to their children why they were being taken away and who were unable to visit with their children in jail for whatever reasons did not see them again until they could have visitors in prison. The elapsed time from their arrest to this first visit could be as short as a few days or weeks to as long as several months.

Plans to Live with Children

As in previous studies, most of the inmate-mothers (88 percent) planned to live with their children upon release. Slightly less than half (49 percent) of these women planned to live with their children within a month after release. Many of them had placed their children with relatives or friends and foresaw no major difficulties in taking charge of the children. Another third of the mothers planned to wait from three months to a year after release before living with children. These women said they wanted some time to reestablish themselves in a new found freedom before accepting the responsibility of parenthood. Some mothers indicated that their own mothers had suggested that they keep the children until the mother had enough time to "get it together" after release. As one woman remarked, "My mother wants to keep them until I get out, finish school, and get a job. She wants me to get myself together before I take them back."

Some mothers (7 percent) were unsure how soon after release they would live with their children. Many of them pointed out that following release they would live in a work release facility for an as yet unspecified time period. Therefore, they were unsure when they would be able to live with their children. Others (11 percent) either did not plan to live with their children or were uncertain at the time of the interview. Many had not been living with their children prior to incarceration. Some said they did not know whether or not they could regain custody after release.

Whether or not mothers planned to reunite with their children following release was related to whether or not they had lived with children in the past. As one might expect, the mothers of about 97 percent of the children (n = 201) who had lived with them in the past planned to reunite with them upon release. More interesting is the finding that mothers of 89 percent of the children (n = 61) who had not lived with them in the past planned to reunite with them after release. Mothers planned to reunite with children regardless of the number of years to parole eligibility. About half of the 58 mothers on whom data was available would be paroled within two years. However, the other 29 mothers would not be paroled for three, four, or more than five years.

There was no significant relationship between race and whether or not mothers planned to live with children or how soon after release mothers planned to do so. Thus, regardless of race or number of years to parole eligibility, mothers wanted to live with their children rather quickly after release. This kind of enthusiasm for reunion may be inappropriate as mothers will be required to obtain gainful employment or go to school, secure housing, and generally readjust to a more "normal" lifestyle. Adding to that the immediate responsibility of caring for one or more children may substantially increase readjustment pressures directly following release. Moreover, if mothers had not lived with children prior to incarceration, there may be unanticipated problems in developing a new relationship. Further, mothers with a long time to parole eligibility who planned to live with children may not be realistically considering such factors as their children's age or stability of their living situation at the time when they will be released.

Despite the good intentions of these mothers, some very basic issues about the well-being of the children and the potential for positive growth of the mother-child relationship must be considered prior to release in determining whether or not and when mothers and children will reunite following release.

Anticipated Problems in Readjusting to Children Following Release

In readjusting to children following release, mothers generally described two types of problems: those they would face (mother's problems) and those their children would face (children's problems). Mother's problems accounted for about 57 percent of those mentioned and children's problems for about 33 percent.[4]

In terms of children's problems, mothers were concerned that children would outright reject them, not want to live with them, not know or respect them any more because of their involvement in crime and/or because children felt abandoned. The remarks of one mother reflected a common theme of guilt mingled with the child's possible rejection:

> This is the one thing I am afraid of when I go home to them. What I may hear—not now but in later years—"When I needed you, mommie, you weren't there." If I try to chastise them and say, "Don't do this," they may say "Mama, how can you say anything? When I needed you, where were you?"

About 19 percent of the mothers reported that their children might be too dependent upon them once they were reunited. A small but significant relationship was found between race and whether or not mothers felt that the child's dependence on them would be a problem (Table 4.7). White mothers tended to fear this problem more than Black mothers. These mothers thought that their children might cling to them for fear that they might not return once they left the house to go to work or shop. Some mothers even noted that their children watched them or followed them around constantly during visits.

Chief among the mother's problems was concern for regaining parental authority. About 36 percent of the mothers said they might not be able to discipline their children. Some indicated that current caretakers used techniques that they would not use. For example, grandparents were often seen as more lax in their approach; they allowed children privileges mothers could not permit or would not enforce rules as mothers thought they should. Other mothers pointed out that their children would test them to see how much they could "get away with" and that they would have to learn to handle these

TABLE 4.7
Possible Problems in Readjusting to Children Following Release

	Number	Percentage of Mothers Reporting[1]	Percentage of Problems[2]
Children's problems:			
Dependence on Mother[3]	26	19	9
May not want to live with me	21	15	8
May not know me	15	11	6
May not respect me	14	10	5
May reject me	13	9	5
Subtotal	89		33
Mother's problems:			
Discipline	49	36	18
Regaining custody[4]	30	22	11
Finding housing	30	22	11
May not relate to children	20	15	7
General readjustment	20	15	7
Relocating children	9	7	3
Subtotal	158		57
Probably no problems	28	20	10
Total	275		100

1. Total percentage exceeds 100.0 percent because some mothers mentioned more than one problem. The denominator for percentages in this column is 138, the number of mothers interviewed.
2. The denominator for percentages in this column is 275, the total number of problems mentioned.
3. Relationship between regaining custody and Race: $r = 0.169$, $p = 0.03$.
4. Relationship between dependence and Race: $r = 0.185$, $p = 0.02$.

situations effectively and fairly. Nearly 15 percent of the mothers, many of whom had been incarcerated for more than two years, said that simply relating to children after minimal contact for so long would be difficult. Over time their children would have changed considerably and initial communications probably would be strained.

Other anticipated mother's problems centered on more practical matters such as regaining custody, relocating children, or finding housing. There was a small but significant correlation between race and whether or not mothers felt that regaining custody would be a problem after release (Table 4.7). White mothers were more concerned about regaining custody than Black mothers. This result may reflect that children of White mothers were more frequently placed with caretakers they did not know. The aura of uncertainty commonly associated with not knowing the whereabouts or care provided to children undoubtedly contributed to this result. Many mothers feared that caretakers would be unwilling to return their children. A few mothers, mainly those whose children lived with foster parents, had little or no idea where the children were located, or how to contact them either during or following incarceration. Rather than pinpoint specific problems, some mothers simply felt that they would face overall adjustment problems. Simultaneously taking on the responsibilities of parenthood and readjusting to the freeworld, they thought, could create temporary pressures.

Over all, these data indicate that mothers perceive possible readjustment problems but generally believe that they are resolvable. Mothers overwhelmingly want to reestablish relationships with their children and feel capable of doing so. They tend to believe that fears or problems will be worked out together with their children.[5]

Summary

These data provide an overview of the psychological consequences of the separation for inmate-mothers generally. In addition, they suggest some interesting differences in perceptions of the separation by race of mother.

With respect to the variations by race, distinctions in the family milieu from which mothers came may at least partially explain these differences in perceptions of the separation. The kinship and extended-family network, more commonly associated with Black families, may in some ways assist inmate-mothers during the separation. An extended family implies that more than just the immediate family members live in close proximity to one another. Children may thus grow up with aunts, uncles, or cousins as easily as with fathers, mothers, or siblings. In terms of handling children, if the mother is unavailable, someone else may care for the children, and the transition of the children from mother to grandmother during the mother's incarceration may be done fairly easily.

Evidence for this extended-family concept among Black but not among White families stems from the fact that caretakers of Black more than White children tended to be the mother's parents. Black mothers also reported more satisfaction with these arrangements than White mothers, whose children often lived with strangers. Prior to incarceration, children of Black mothers who did not live with them were more likely than White children to live with the woman's parents or other relatives nearby; White children, again, more often lived with nonrelatives. In terms of legal custody, more Black than White mothers retained custody during the separation, perhaps because the mother's parent had offered simply to care for the child in the mother's absence.

Similarly, when custody had been relinquished, more White than Black mothers indicated that they had been coerced into giving it up. Black mothers had voluntarily given up custody mainly when there were few or no relatives to whom they could turn for assistance. Thus, many Black mothers felt there was no other alternative to provide adequate care for children. Some Black mothers did indicate that their own mothers forced them to give up their children because, as one woman commented, "She didn't think my lifestyle was suitable for raising children." Given that more White than Black mothers relinquished custody, it is no surprise that more White mothers feared that regaining custody would be an important and difficult problem following release.

The extended-family concept may, to some extent, account for the fact that more White than Black mothers feared that their children would be too dependent upon them following release. If children may easily move around from one family member to another, in visiting, living, or seeking nurturance and guidance, mothers may not feel so pressured as the sole family member for social support. When there are few, if any, additional family members available, as with White inmate-mothers, mothers may indeed feel this pressure and fear their children will look almost totally to them for support upon release.

In terms of emotional reactions to the separation, regardless of race, mothers generally expressed feelings of inadequacy, despondency, and fear of loss of their children. As several mothers aptly summarized the impact of the separation on themselves, "You can't be a mother and be in prison."

Yet, the data indicate that despite the feelings of inadequacy, most mothers want to maintain ties and reunite with their children following release. Several findings support this point. For one thing, prior to incarceration most children lived with their mothers. Living situations reportedly were separate from other relatives in many cases. This finding suggests that mothers were required to be responsible for their children at that time. However, the data compiled thus far in this and other studies provide no information as to the quality of the mother-child relationship prior to arrest. One facet of this relationship worth exploring is the extent to and conditions under which there may have been some form of role reversal such that children have acted as the parents for mothers.

For most women and children, regardless of race, the current incarceration is the first major separation from one another. One mother even had her teenage children drive her to the institution in order to be with them as long as possible immediately prior to the lengthy separation.

About half of the mothers retained legal custody despite the separation. Some mothers voluntarily gave up custody on a temporary basis because they believed the children would benefit more with a nonincarcerated guardian. Whether or not mothers gave up custody voluntarily, they uniformly wanted to regain it upon release. However, many mothers expressed grave concern about the likelihood of doing so given their status as ex-felons.

At some point, most mothers had told their children that they were going to be incarcerated. Although they may not have blatantly said, "I am going to prison," most mothers in some way conveyed the information that they were going away to be punished for bad behavior. This finding suggests that imprisoned mothers want to be honest with their children; they feel children have a right to know or are capable of understanding the circumstances of the separation. In fact, mothers who had not had the opportunity to explain their absence worried that their children would receive misleading information from others and perhaps lose respect for them. Taken collectively, these results suggest that, regardless of race, mothers want to stay in touch with their children during incarceration and that they say, at least, that they want to resume responsibility for their children following release.

The lack of daily contact with children and the consequent loss of parenting skills coupled with feelings of inadequacy to reassert parental authority may make this desire for reunion shortly after release an unrealistic goal. The sense of inadequacy so often expressed by inmate-mothers may be closely linked with both the way in which these women view themselves (self-concept) and their attitudes about raising children. Since both self-concept and child-rearing attitudes may influence the way in which inmate-mothers respond to their children following release, each of these factors must be examined in terms of the separation.

Notes

1. In terms of the number of months spent in jails in the past, only 26 of the 284 (9 percent) women had spent from one month to a year in jails. Because of the small number of women in this category, these data were not broken out by the race of

the mothers. However, even assuming that all 26 of these women who had served time in jails were mothers, only 14 percent (n = 190) of the mothers in the study would fall into this category. The point is that, again, this small proportion suggests that there has been minimal separation from children in the past because of incarceration.

2. Differential responses to questions regarding legal custody of children suggests that some inmate-mothers may not be certain whether or not they do, in fact, still have custody of their children. In any case, future research efforts in this area should carefully explore inmate-mothers' understanding of their legal rights to children.

3. Additional data support the notion that mothers want to honestly tell their children about their absence. Independent ratings of taped interviews by one other person indicated that 71 percent of the 92 mothers rated had wanted to tell their children the truth.

4. The remaining 10 percent of the problems are accounted for by the fact that some mothers (n = 28) did not anticipate any problems in readjusting to their children after release.

5. This overwhelming positive attitude towards their ability to readjust to the freeworld and the maternal role simultaneously was reflected in responses to the question how much confidence inmate-mothers felt in resuming parental responsibilities. There was no significant relationship between expressed level of confidence and race. About 93 percent of all mothers (90 percent of the 77 White mothers and 97 percent of the 61 Black mothers on whom data were obtained) reported that they were confident, very confident, or extremely confident in doing so. The question that remains to be tested is the extent to which this expressed confidence realistically indicates positive, effective parenting skills which will be used in dealing with children upon release.

5

Self-Concept and Child-Rearing Attitudes

"Self" theory posits that the "self is the frame of reference through which an individual interacts with his world" (Fitts et al. 1971:3). In this sense, the individual synthesizes input from the outside world and forms a response to it. The way in which a woman sees herself, therefore, plays an important role in the way that she responds to others. Moreover, the way in which a woman sees herself is determined, in part, by the way in which others interact with and see her. Thus, one might expect women in prison to see themselves rather negatively because of the stigma of the crime and social ostracism.

One might expect that if involvement with children forms an "axis of self-esteem" (Lundberg et al. 1975) for inmate-mothers, then these women may view themselves even less favorably than nonmothers. The fact that they were to a large extent responsible for the separation could depress the way in which inmate-mothers see themselves. Therefore, understanding the way in which women in prison, inmate-mothers in particular, view themselves may provide some useful insights into how they respond to and interpret their environment.

The child-rearing attitudes expressed by a mother may be indicative of the way in which she interacts with her children. These behavior patterns may, in turn, affect the personality development of the child. Therefore, it is important to understand parental attitudes towards raising children (Shoeben 1949; Schaefer and Bell 1958; Pumroy 1966). For mothers in prison who rarely see their children on a day-to-day basis, however, child-rearing attitudes may bear no relationship to the ways in which they respond to children after release. Yet, these attitudes have utility in other ways. First, they provide another means to understand how inmate-mothers see themselves in the parenting role and how they see their children. Second, for those who wish to help inmate-mothers plan how to handle children effectively upon release, child-rearing attitudes during incarceration provide a starting point for discussion and assistance.

With these points in mind, the self-concept and child-rearing attitudes of inmate-mothers were assessed. In order to measure these concepts, the Tennessee Self Concept Scale (TSCS) and Maryland Parent Attitude Survey (MPAS) were used.[1]

Level of Self-Concept

The way in which women inmates perceived themselves was not related to motherhood—mothers and nonmothers alike held a generally low but normal view of themselves (Table 5.1).[2] Women in prison generally tended to express the lowest levels of confidence about their identities (Who am I?) and about their own behavior (What am I doing?). They expressed the highest levels of confidence about their acceptance of themselves (the extent to which they live up to their own expectations of themselves) and, to a somewhat lesser extent, about their view of themselves physically and personally (feelings of self-worth).

Incarcerated women in this study tended to have a very healthy openness to criticism of themselves, though they expressed a great deal of contradiction and confusion in terms of who they are. They showed poor controls over their own behavior, tended to be impulsive, to "act out" their feelings, and to be easily influenced by others. In this sense, they more often seemed to employ external than internal means to define themselves.

Given that they have been ostracized by society, perhaps rejected by their own families, and consigned to a world of relative isolation and emptiness, it is not surprising that these women should be uncertain of themselves and their relationship with others. Moreover, prisons tend to foster dependency among women on external sources. These characteristics of uncertainty and inconsistencies in self-concept are common among female delinquents (Fitts and Hamner 1969).

Although the general nature of responses in this study parallels that of women inmates in other studies using the Tennessee Self Concept Scale, what seems to be uncommon is that the overall level of self-concept among inmates in the present study is slightly higher than in previous studies. In particular, women inmates in the present study tended to accept themselves and their behaviors somewhat more than their counterparts in previous research. They were more satisfied with their relationship to God, their feelings of being a "good" person, their sense of personal self-worth, their value as a family member, and their interactions with others in general.[3]

What accounts for these differences is difficult to determine. More favorable circumstances in the prison setting or in the testing situation may have some effect. The institutions that were selected for study were chosen because of their inclusion of programs to retain ties with children. This may reflect some progressive trends in correctional treatment that were absent earlier. However, a determination of the effectiveness of any treatment program to enhance self-

TABLE 5.1
The Relationship between Tennessee Self Concept Scale (TSCS)
Scores and Other Factors

TSCS Scores	Correlation	Significance	n
Total Positive Score and:			
Motherhood of inmates	-.07	p = .312	195
Age at first misdemeanor conviction	.22	p = .02	137
Time to parole eligibility from date of admission	.15	p = .04	137
Sentence length imposed	.25	p = .002	133
Family Self and:			
Motherhood of inmates	-.05	p = .468	195
Frequency of phone calls to children	.23	p = .0035	137
Frequency of correspondence with children	.32	p = .0001	135
Level of confidence as mother	-.31[1]	p = .0001	137
Guilt about crime	-.28	p = .003	112
Insecurity about relationship with children	-.21	p = .02	117

1. This negative correlation indicates that responses to this item were presented in reverse order so that 1 = Extremely Confident and 5 = Not Confident at all.

concept requires careful measurement of this construct prior to and following program participation.

Although it is inappropriate to compare different measures of self-concept, it is appropriate to consider similarities in overall conclusions. The general finding that women inmates tend to feel relatively positive about themselves was also obtained in the National Study of Women's Correctional Programs.

Glick and Neto (1977:171) found that "the majority of women scored in the direction of high self-esteem" on two-thirds of the items used. That incarcerated women see themselves somewhat positively runs counter to common assumptions that imprisoned women are totally self-effacing, self-denigrating individuals. However, in the present as in the previous studies that used the same instrument to measure self-concept, low positive scores suggest a need to provide both the environment and programmatic components to enable these women to unify and raise their view of themselves considerably.

Relationship of Self-Concept to Other Factors

The extent to which inmate-mothers viewed themselves was not affected by background characteristics (age, race, marital status, job before prison, number of children) and most criminal history factors (age at first adjudication delinquent, number of prior misdemeanors and felony convictions, nature of present offense of conviction). As shown in Table 5.1, women who had been convicted of their first misdemeanor later in life were more positive and confident about themselves than women who had been convicted of their first misdemeanor in their late teens or early twenties. These results suggest that early involvement in the criminal justice system as an adult has a detrimental effect on the way in which a woman sees herself and that this self-assessment carries over with additional criminal involvement.

The length of time a woman spends behind bars may be expected to influence the way in which she sees herself. We might expect that the longer she is in prison and away from her family, the less favorably she sees herself. However, in the present study the opposite was found: inmate-mothers who had a longer time to parole eligibility from the date of admission to prison or who had been given a longer sentence saw themselves more favorably. This result suggests that women who have more time to serve tend to make the most of the situation, to become adjusted to their plight, and perhaps begin to define themselves positively in terms of their surroundings. In this sense, these mothers may become more institutionalized than women serving shorter sentences.

The way in which inmate-mothers viewed themselves in relation to their family was related to such factors as communication with children, overall level of confidence as a mother, and the extent of guilt and insecurity expressed during the interview. Women who corresponded with their children or frequently called them by phone felt more favorable about their relationships with their family. Similarly, women who expressed a high degree of confidence about their ability to resume the maternal role and foresaw fewer problems in reuniting with children also saw themselves and their relationships to family members in a positive light. On the other hand, mothers who expressed a great deal of guilt about the crime or who were concerned that the relationships with their children might totally collapse during imprisonment felt fairly negative about themselves and their family relationships (see Table 5.1).

Child-Rearing Attitudes

Inmate-mothers generally expressed attitudes of protectiveness and indulgence towards their children.[4] They favored minimal punishment and only when it is absolutely necessary. These mothers rarely outwardly rejected their children. Their child-rearing attitudes included the following specific characteristics.

Protectiveness

Inmate-mothers expressed very protective attitudes towards their children. They wanted their children to take a minimum of risks. Consequently, they tended to be overly watchful and to cautiously assess dangerous aspects of various situations. They felt, for instance, that they should take children to and from school to minimize the possibility of harm. They wanted to hide dangerous objects and to leave a night light on for children to avoid any discomfort or possible accidents in the dark. Moreover, they wanted to be involved in making decisions for the children and to do things for them even though they might be capable themselves. They rarely wanted to push their children to achieve beyond their capabilities and did not try to force them to grow up quickly.

Indulgence

Inmate-mothers expressed a great deal of warmth and affection towards their children and tended to overlook shortcomings. They expressed the desire to shower their children with gifts and toys, to provide them with the very best of everything, and to plan surprise parties for them. Further, they did not want to force children to do things against their will, such as picking up toys or working around the house. In this sense, they expressed a laxness in attitudes towards disciplining children.

Disciplinarian

Mothers who showed stronger disciplinarian tendencies also tended to demand that children obey immediately when asked and said that they tended to use more physical punishment in disciplining children on the outside. More protective mothers were less inclined to use physical punishment on the outside in disciplining their children (Table 5.2).

TABLE 5.2
Pearson's Correlations for MPAS Scores and Other Factors

MPAS Scale Factor	Correlation	Significance	n
Disciplinarian By:			
Demands immediate obedience	.24	p = .010	101
Use of physical punishment outside	.23	p = .020	97
Protectiveness by:			
Use of physical punishment outside	-.25	p = .010	97
Rejecting by:			
Anger that own behavior caused separation	.21	p = .025	111
TSCS Scores:			
Total Positive	-.31	p = .001	137
Identity	-.24	p = .004	137
Acts	-.33	p = .001	137
Physical self	-.20	p = .020	137
Moral/ethical self	-.23	p = .009	137
Personal self	-.25 ·	p = .003	137
Family self	-.22	p = .010	137
Social self	-.30	p = .001	137
Self-criticism	-.31	p = .001	137

Rejection

In contrast with their protectiveness, inmate-mothers expressed very little open and active hostility towards their children. They generally preferred to have children around them rather than out of the way watching television or asleep. In this sense, they were far from seeing children as an inconvenience to be tolerated. Moreover, they very rarely rejected their children based more upon their own feelings than upon the child's behavior. However, those mothers who expressed the greatest anger about the separation because of their own behavior tended to reject their children as well. Interestingly, inmate-mothers who tended to be more rejecting of their children also tended to have less confidence in themselves and in their relationships with their family and friends (Table 5.2.).

Summary

Taken together, the results on self-concept suggest that women in prison, whether or not they are mothers, generally have a low but somewhat favorable view of themselves. For inmate-mothers in particular, conviction of their first misdemeanor at a fairly early age in adulthood affected the way in which they viewed themselves. Many of these women had given birth to their first child as unwed mothers by age 16. The juxtaposition of initiation into motherhood and involvement in the criminal justice process almost simultaneously may have jointly reinforced a low self-image.

In addition, inmate-mothers who were able to communicate with their children by letter or phone on a regular basis had a somewhat more favorable view of their family relationships than those who feared that the separation jeopardized family relationships. These data suggest that concern for relationships with children may indeed affect the way in which inmate-mothers see themselves and that regular contacts with children may enhance positive self-perceptions.

Child-rearing attitudes are useful for understanding how inmate-mothers see their relationships with their children and their own role as a parent. The findings in the present study suggest that, as parents, these women tend to be very accepting of their children's behaviors and highly protective of them. They want to lavish excessive warmth, affection, and guidance upon their children and to punish them minimally.

This seemingly ideal approach to parenthood is not surprising, given the inmate-mothers' lack of continuous contact with children. Further, inmate-mothers' misgivings about handling discipline, expressed in the interviews, is in line with their more lenient attitude towards disciplining children. These results suggest, however, that inmate-mothers may need some assistance in balancing out their approaches to children. Love and affection are, of course, important; but overprotectiveness may impair the children's development as independently functioning persons. In not being allowed to make mistakes, children may be prevented from learning on their own.

Parenting programs for inmate-mothers might, therefore, use child-rearing attitudes as a yardstick against which to measure progress in achieving a more balanced perspective on raising children. The child-rearing attitudes an inmate-mother takes with her when she leaves the prison may well form the foundation for her interactions with her children.

Finally, the tendency of women in prison, and inmate-mothers in particular, to identify themselves in terms of external rather than internal factors may be a function of the prison environment. Prisons unintentionally foster a sense of dependency because they restrict individual initiative and involvement in decision making. For inmate-mothers, a greater sense of independence might be developed through more direct decision making about their children beyond simply placement during incarceration. A mother who cares about her child may develop a more integrated sense of self as well as responsible decision-making skills through involvement with her child during imprisonment.

Notes

1. A discussion of the rationale for selection of the Tennessee Self Concept Scale and Maryland Parent Attitude Survey is included in Appendix A.
2. What is meant by saying that there is a "low but normal" self-concept is that the overall view that inmate-mothers in this study have of themselves falls within the cutoff points for a normal self-perception that were determined in the development of the Tennessee Self Concept Scale initially. For the overall concept, these limits are 421 and 319. The mean score for the inmates in the present study was 330. Therefore, the average score for the inmates in this study falls within the limits but at the lower-end; a high score reflects a more positive self-concept. The score for the norm group was closer to 350. Individual scale scores measuring identity, acceptance, behavior, physical self, moral/ethical self, personal self, family self and social self fell within normal limits but below the scores for the norm group. (See Fitts 1965:20 for norm limits for each scale.)
3. See Appendix B for specific Tennessee Self Concept Scale scores of incarcerated women in this study compared with those of imprisoned women in two earlier studies.
4. The means and standard deviations of 128 inmate-mothers in the study for the Maryland Parent Attitude Survey included the following. On the disciplinarian scale, scores had a mean of 21.8 and standard deviation of 5.8. On the indulgent scale, scores had a mean of 23.2 and standard deviation of 8.9. On the protective scale, scores had a mean of 28.8 and standard deviation of 3.8. On the rejecting scale, scores had a mean of 14.1 and standard deviation of 5.8. Further research should explore the nature of the differences in child-rearing attitudes between carefully selected samples of incarcerated and nonincarcerated mothers.

6

Inmate-Mothers and Drugs: A Schizophrenic Lifestyle

As the previous chapters indicate, inmate-mothers tend to have a low but positive self-concept, express shame and guilt at the reasons for the separation from their children, and feel inadequate about resuming parental authority upon release. For those inmate-mothers who had been involved with drugs prior to incarceration, there is an extra burden added to an already guilt-laden self-perception. These mothers have not only the stigma of being convicted of crimes and separated from their children but also of being labeled as potheads, pushers, and perhaps prostitutes.[1]

There is little research on the psychological consequences of drug involvement on mothers or on the mother-child relationship. Most studies tend to deal with the effects of drugs on neonates or fetuses rather than on the mother. As Colten (1980:2) contended, the mothers are viewed as the "independent variable—as the source and never the victim of the problem—and seen only in the most negative terms." In order to reverse this trend, Colten ascertained feelings about mothering and self-perceptions among addicted and nonaddicted mothers. She found that addicted mothers overwhelmingly expressed more inadequacy in the maternal role than nonaddicted mothers (ibid.:16).

To date there has been no similar research on inmate-mothers.[2] Yet, in conjunction with the shame and despair associated with the separation because of incarceration, involvement with drugs can only heighten the sense of inadequacy. Given the paucity of research on drug involvement as it relates to relationships with children prior to imprisonment, this chapter highlights some of the dominant themes about drug use discussed by inmate-mothers during the interviews. It is important to shed some light on problems in the mother-child relationship brought about by drug involvement, in order to deal effectively with them in any systematic program to maintain or reestablish ties among inmate-mothers and children.

With these points in mind, this chapter considers a number of issues: inmate-mothers' motivations for drug involvement; the impact drug use has had on their drug involvement; how they perceive their children; the mechanisms used in explaining drug involvement; and the explanations inmate-mothers offered children for their drug-related behavior.

Of the 126 inmate-mothers who participated in the taped portion of the interviews, 55 (43.6 percent) indicated that they had sold and/or used drugs or had been alcoholics prior to their current incarceration. As there were only 3 women who were admittedly alcoholics, the chapter deals primarily with inmate-mothers and drugs; however, information from inmate-mothers who had been alcoholics is presented and noted.

Motivations for Drug Involvement

Research on drug use among adults suggests a number of motivations for involvement including physical/sensory stimulation, tension release, socializing, rebellion, remaining alert, aesthetic appreciation, increasing meaning in life, and creating adventure (Bowker 1978:71). In addition, women are often introduced to drugs through males with whom they feel a close personal relationship and through friends (ibid.:63, 70). These patterns of motivation and initial involvement with drugs were characteristic of inmate-mothers interviewed.

Some mothers indicated that a significant other, most notably male, had introduced them to drugs. For instance, a 25-year-old White mother said:

> My ex-husband got me started into it—got me addicted. I had been in drugs about two years on the streets. I started smoking. He was heavier into drugs when I first met him. He was a drug addict. I wanted to change him but it didn't work. He changed me. He would wake up sick and ask me to go to a doctor to get him these pills that he was on—that he was going to detox himself. I believed him.

> I have always said I would never stick a needle in my arm. And he would talk me into doing downs and things like that. I kind of liked the feeling—the drugged feeling—you would get. And then after awhile he talked me into shooting some dope, "Come on. Try it, you'll like it." And once he saw that I liked it he would push harder for me to go out to the doctor's to get more stuff. When I saw I was addicted I was really upset.

> I knew I was addicted because I woke up one morning and thought I had the flu. I was aching all over. My nose was running; my eyes were watering. He was trying to get me up to go to the doctor. When I told him how I felt he told me I was addicted. He said, "Come over here and I will prove it to you." I got a shot. As soon as I was up I didn't hurt at all. My eyes cleared up and everything.

Still another 22-year-old mother, who began experimenting with drugs at age 13 hinted at the importance of drugs for her relationship with her boy friend:

> When we first got together I told him—he didn't have a job—that if he got a job I'd stand by him. I told him if he decided to be a thief I'd stand by him. We both went into drugs together. I went into it on my own. I am strong headed. He didn't make me get into it.

Other mothers whose friends included users and dealers found drugs a socially acceptable means of escaping reality:

> I started shooting heroin when I was 12 years old. I moved in with my sister and I had a lot of freedom. My friends were doing it and they never pressured me into doing it. I did it because it felt good. I had a lot of problems at the time. I knew they did and they would shoot drugs and it would all be all right. So I did it and my problems just went away so I just kept doing it and eventually I got a habit. I always told myself that I am not going to be as bad as that guy or that guy and I was getting real bad

Some of these women noted further how easy access to drugs encouraged their use as a retreat from everyday pressures:

> I knew a lot of people that were dealing in drugs and I didn't have to pay a majority of times. So I got hooked real easy. . . . It was a need to escape from problems, from pressures, from things I had to deal with. My husband had an alcohol problem. As a matter of fact, the whole five years we lived together he never knew about my drug problem, that I was strung out. I used to keep the books and he never was aware of where the money went. I guess a lot of the reasons I got involved is that I had it easy, as far as my access to drugs. I ended up getting hooked and it went from bad to worse.

For some mothers, over time, using drugs had become a natural part of their lifestyle as a coping mechanism. One 32-year-old Black mother who had been using drugs for about fifteen years said she first began taking them when she lived at home, to help her contend with her home life situation.

> It was hard. You have to understand the family structure first. First we were all together and then I moved out and saw them on weekends. I had to do something to tolerate . . . the garbage I was receiving from my parents—my mother. I was just running and dope is what I ran into. It was all I had. She would start the crap and just keep going. I don't know if I can say she forced me into the drugs but . . . I just wanted something.

Some inmate-mothers became addicted to prescribed drugs in adulthood, as this 34-year-old mother of a nine-year-old boy indicated:

My son really didn't know I was on drugs. There were so many times I was in the hospital for it. But then I was in the hospital for nervous breakdowns and deep depressions too. I was in there for a month at a time. One of the drugs did it because I would take it to get rid of the headaches. But after awhile I would get high on the pills. So I would take more and more of it. And it helped me because me and my husband were having trouble. And it helped me to cope with that.

Eventually her habit led her into calling in prescriptions fraudulently:

I called in two prescriptions to the drug store. I had been on this medicine for so long and I couldn't sleep or anything . . . the headaches were driving me nuts. I really needed something. There was no shrink where I lived and the doctor I was going to would not give this to me. So I called in the prescriptions and the police picked me up.

Drug-dependent inmate-mothers in this study who had been prostitutes said that they had done so primarily as a means of support. They often began their "career" early in adolescence and later started using drugs as a response to "on-the-job" pressures. For instance, one Black 22-year-old mother of an 8-year-old son indicated that she

needed money and I didn't have a good education. I had to quit school when I was young because I was pregnant. I needed some support and couldn't keep a job I didn't like so I thought I could do something easy. But it's not easy to be a prostitute.

In terms of her initiation into both prostitution and drugs she noted:

I didn't do much real hard. I used to smoke a lot of pot. I never was a junkie but used to shoot drugs. I never got strung out on them. . . . I think it was the environment that I was in for me to start messing with drugs. As far as the prostitution thing I just got into it. I never thought I would get into it. I used to laugh at everybody else who would be standing on the street corners. It was kind of a shock to me to get into it. . . . I guess I wanted to. It was so hip and cool and once I got into it, it was hard to get out of it.

Another inmate-mother said she "got involved in prostitution at an early age because of the money." Her drug taking began with smoking pot and popping speed pills to stay alert. As she put it:

With the life I was leading, I needed it. I had to have something to keep me going so I started out on speed. Then I went to cocaine. I messed with heroin for awhile. But that was a downer. I had to have something to keep me going. Coke and speed kept me going.

These motivations for drug involvement among inmate-mothers parallel those among mothers in general: a need to escape reality or to cope with problems; experimentation; coaxing by a significant other; remaining alert; or addiction to prescriptions. However, the added responsibility of children tends to both interfere with drug involvement and to make drug involvement an interference with the mother-child relationship.

Effects of Drug Use on Relationships with Children

During the interviews, a striking response was an initial denial that drug involvement had any direct effect upon relationships with children. However, as each interview progressed, mothers more willingly admitted that the drug involvement clashed with their desires to function effectively as mothers. For instance, at the outset of the discussion, one woman said she was able to handle children and drugs simultaneously:

> It just fit. When I was out I was on drugs. Really I wasn't in my right mind half the time. Lots of things I should have thought about I didn't even think about because I was ripping and running. But I would have the evenings to spend with my son because I would always do what I had to do during the day. He just felt I was going to work and coming back and of course I didn't tell him any different.

As the discussion continued, it became clear that this woman, as so many others, was living a schizophrenic lifestyle—junkie by day and mother by night, or visa versa. This delicately balanced equilibrium could be offset at any moment by additional pressures. Consequently, an ever-present self-doubt that belied the apparent coolness emerged as a dominant theme in many of the mothers' remarks. This same woman said later in the interview:

> More or less having to come home and be a mother to him and then still being on drugs and during the day hustling—doing what I had to do to get the money for drugs. I was kind of living two lives. . . . It's very difficult. And I couldn't deal with it because if I could have dealt with it, I probably wouldn't be here today.

> But it was hard for me to deal with it. Emotionally it did have some effects on me. I thought I was being a mother for him and doing everything for him and taking care of his needs and everything. But when you really look at it, I don't know, maybe I wasn't. I don't know. I think I was there for him when he needed me a majority of the time.

> But sometimes I would take him to my mother's house and then go out and get some more drugs. He would never be subjected to any of it as far as the drugs go. I really don't feel that I was the mother I should have been, that I could have been if it hadn't been for the drugs in my life. And I just couldn't

handle the situation. I felt that I needed the drugs. Maybe it is something inside of me that I need to get out. I don't know.

For this woman, drugs had a very definite impact on the relationship with her son. It divided the time she could spend with him and amplified guilt about her behavior. In the same way, other mothers said they could handle the relationship with their children, until the drugs took control. At that point, the relationship diminished and guilt intensified. One young mother repeatedly remarked how guilty she felt that her drug dependence detracted from her relationship with her daughter:

I got to the point where my daughter would want to do things like go to the park and I would say to her I have to run here. I had to take care of myself first and I used to feel really guilty about it. It is not that I didn't want to do those things with her but it was that I was a sick person and if I didn't get it I would be even sicker. So I had to go out and take care of that first.

Then after I would do drugs, I would feel even guiltier about it. I neglected her. Sometimes I would come home and she would be asleep. I always tried to take care of it in the day. But I couldn't always do that.

Then before all this happened [her crime] I checked myself into a hospital to detox myself. I had a lot of trouble with my friends calling me in the hospital and I was in the worst stages. I wasn't taking anything. I was just locked in a room. They would call me and tell me they had pills if I wanted some. Two days later I ended up here—trying to get a prescription filled. It's crazy. I know I never wanted to use drugs.

And I definitely know I will have to start a relationship with my daughter all over again because towards the end it was getting bad. . . . I feel like I've let her down in a lot of ways and I think she senses this because before I started doing drugs I would do things with her like go to the park or take her on the tennis court with me. After awhile, I neglected doing all these things with her and it makes me feel bad. I feel like it will take awhile to establish a relationship again. I feel guilty about it.

Inmate-mothers who had been prostitutes and had used drugs had still another complicating factor in their relationships with their children. Frequently they said that the "fast" life made it difficult to care for children. One Black 28-year-old mother had begun working the streets at age 12 and had continued in this way off and on throughout her life until she was incarcerated. Because of her youth and lifestyle, her three youngest children had spent the first five years of their lives with her own mother. At age 19 she was determined to live with her children. She quit taking drugs and began working two steady jobs back to back. With the pressures of this schedule she again started using speed to "keep up." Averaging fewer than four hours of sleep a night for jobs that provided less income than prostitution eventually forced her to return to street life. However, she kept all of her children. Of her return to prostitution she said:

> It's hard being a dancer and working late at night, especially to have time with my kids. . . . I was really going. When you take speed you are constantly going. I was killing myself really. In the day when I wanted to take a nap, I had to take a downer—smoke a joint—to let me relax. I would doze off when the kids would take their nap because when they got back up, they had a lot of energy.
>
> I took them to the parks in the day. But I had to have money so I went out. I didn't mean to make it my life; I didn't enjoy what I did. But I knew I had to do it to keep up with the expenses I had.

The conflict and guilt characteristic of inmate-mothers who had used drugs was a recurrent theme throughout this young mother's encapsulation of her life. Although she expressed concern for her children, her street-life survival was bound up in drug dependence. Consequently, this woman's lifestyle, as that of many other inmate-mothers in this study who had used drugs and/or worked the streets, became a vicious cycle, an almost futile attempt to link together the pills and diapers of her world into a cohesive, unified whole. The net result of this effort was an intensive guilt exacerbated by conviction and incarceration for a crime that may have been unrelated to the prior lifestyle.

One consequence of this sense of guilt was a feeling of ineffectiveness in disciplining children. Because of their involvement with drugs, these mothers often admitted their inability to exert parental authority even when it was warranted. As one mother said:

> As far as her obeying me, it got to the point where she would not obey me any more like she used to. Because I would tell her to do something. She would be hesitant about doing it and I saw it too. Naturally, I couldn't whip her for it because I felt guilty myself. Whereas, before the drugs, I could say to her to do something and she was always cheerful about it. . . . I felt too guilty about it to try to correct her for it because I was too . . . well, I felt like it wasn't her, it was me.

Thus, over and above the potential problems in handling discipline because of incarceration, inmate-mothers who had used drugs often felt an additional concern; how to recapture the credibility and confidence as a parent which had evaporated even before the separation?

Mechanisms to Explain Drug Use and Children's Perceived Reactions

The mechanisms used by inmate-mothers to explain their drug involvement ranged from attempts to explain it to denial and flat rejection that children could understand it.

Those inmate-mothers who wanted to be truthful expressed concern that their children understand the consequences of taking drugs for their own lives. One mother commented:

> He has already asked me about drugs. He saw me with my eyes open and he asked me if I was sick. . . . I said, "I have a drug problem." And . . . how do you explain it to a three year old child?

> If he starts asking me about drugs, I am not going to tell him no because then I'd be a hypocrite. He could throw that back at me that I did it. I'll say, "This is what it does to you and this is what can happen. It's your decision." I don't want to lie about it. I will tell him what has taken place in my life.

Alternatively, as this 28-year-old mother of two boys admitted, some mothers were so caught up in drugs that they remained insensitive to children's recognition of their problem until they acknowledged it as a problem for themselves:

> The hardest thing for me to acknowledge was the fact that I am a dope fiend. It took me nearly a year to acknowledge that fact. My family knew it. . . . I am sure that they were aware of it, though I was blind to the fact. They never saw me with a syringe. They were around me when I would smoke weed. They have seen me out of it several times. They even brought it to me. At the time, I was not in any position to talk with them about it. Even for as much love as I have had for my kids at the time.

> Still, I look at myself in the past as a very selfish person because I was being insensitive to their needs. From that I can imagine the changes I was putting them through. Whereas, now they see me and they can talk about the past and they say, "Mommie wasn't right at the time." I can explain to them that I had a drug problem and that I wasn't right at the time and they can tell me where they will help me and that makes me feel good. I never really sat down and totally explained to them. I was very insensitive to them. I was hurting them and not even realizing it.

The most common response, however, was to try to hide the drug problem from children entirely. Usually, inmate-mothers said that they tried to take care of their drug needs when children were not around. The reasons for this behavior were as varied as the women themselves. Some women were concerned that their children not see them if they felt they would be unable to handle the situation. As one mother said:

> I never have him around when there are drugs around because I never know if I am going to be able to handle it—both me and the other people.

Some mothers wanted to avoid the embarrassment of trying to explain drug use to their children. Others sought to avert probing questions and pleas that children be allowed to try drugs for themselves. Still other mothers saw their drug habit as their own problem and not that of their children. For whatever reasons, inmate-mothers uniformly said that they did not want their children exposed to a life of drugs.

Women used a variety of mechanisms to avoid children's discovery of their drug use. Some mothers used drugs when children had gone off to school or were safely tucked in bed. Other mothers would not have drugs in their homes but went to a friend's house instead. For instance, one mother, who said that she felt uneasy about "doing drugs" around her 4-year-old-son, attended to her drug needs elsewhere:

> I never had it in my house. I always went to one of their houses. I had a girl friend with no kids and her own place. I would go there and do my drugs and come home to him. He was never around it. I never did have it around him. I wouldn't even have it in my own house.

> My son never saw me strung out. Well, he was at the age that he really didn't know. Drugs didn't really change me as far as the way I acted towards my son. It was still the same love and affection. I did everything for him he needed. I was with him in the evenings. It was just during the day I was on it, when he was in the nursery. He had everything he wanted and he never knew I was on drugs. He didn't have any reason to suspect I was on drugs because he was never around them.

A few inmate-mothers, particularly those under twenty-five years old at the time of the interview who had given birth to their first child in their early teens, preferred to have their own mothers raise their children. Like this 20-year-old mother of a 3-year-old child, some mothers considered their own lifestyles unfit for a child:

> My son was not around when I was doing drugs. . . . I had him when I was in the eleventh grade. After that I was intending to complete school and I wasn't even going to school. My mother had him when I was supposed to be in school. . . . I told her to keep him because I didn't like to be under the influence around him, no way. So I let her keep him and I stayed at my own place and just did whatever I wanted to do. That's probably the reason I let my mother have custody of him—I was young when I had him. I just wasn't really ready to settle down.

Similarly, a mother who had given birth to her 8-year-old son at age 13 said that she was not psychologically ready to take on motherhood at that age despite the physical reality; she asked her own mother to care for the child:

> I was running the streets and not ready to settle down and take care of a child. I did love him a great deal but was just too young and wild . . . . I felt that I wasn't able to love him enough. I was really neglecting him. I would take him

over to my parents and have them babysit him for two or three days; I think otherwise he was missing a whole lot.

Inmate-mothers who used drugs at home were plagued with the possibility that their children would discover their secret. When the children found drug paraphernalia or confronted their mothers with questions about their drug behavior, their mothers commonly said that they were sick and had to take medicine. A frequently mentioned malady was diabetes. Since diabetics often use self-injections of insulin, the explanation of diabetes provided an easy excuse for the presence of needle-tracked arms or drug materials at home. Explanations of sickness suggest the importance of denying the drug dependence to children. For instance, a young mother of a 9-year-old girl explained:

> She'd see me when I would go to my girl friend's house. I would shoot it there. But I shot it at home too. She never saw me act crazy or anything but she knew I was in the bathroom a long time. Then she would see blood all over the place because I thought there were bad veins and I would get mad and get started all over the place.

> She asked me who beat me up because I had bruises all over my arms. I didn't explain it to her. I would tell her I fell—anything. . . . I guess she saw me strung out. She knew I was sick. I told her I was diabetic, that I had to take these shots every day. Then when she found the syringe, she didn't say anything about it. She just said "Oh" and that was all.

> And then you think about it and you remember this person and that person— they were so horrible. They did this and they did that and you never think one day it will be you. You know, I would think about people who shoot up. I knew this guy who shot dope and didn't think he was much of a person. And then I did it too.

Typical of a pattern of denial, this woman's comments indicate that despite her attempts to hide her drug habit from her daughter, its grim reality was very salient to her. In this respect, self-doubt and concern with her own behavior and its impacts on her child's perceptions of her as a mother stem from her drug involvement not from her crime. The crime and subsequent separation only further intensify the guilt and shame.

Given the attempts that they thought had been successful to mask the drug involvement, some women said that they were stunned and embarrassed when their children asked them questions about it:

> My [13-year-old] son knew more so than my [9-year-old] daughter. My dad gets into it and says, "It's all your fault." So my son asked me about it: "Will those drugs take you away from us again?" And it knocked me for a loop.

Similarly, a 30-year-old mother who had a 13-year-old daughter was startled when her daughter asked her about her habit. But she tried to explain it:

> She has been around me when I was using drugs. She asked me about it. I had to sit down and tell her that I had a serious problem. The first time I was cooking breakfast one morning and she said to me, "Mommie, you're a junkie, aren't you?" I blushed real hard. I said, "What do you mean a junkie? Where did you hear this?" She said, "Grandma said you're a junkie and you take shots." I said, "I am a junkie and I do take shots. . . . We need to sit down and talk about this because this isn't all there is to that."
>
> I told her that I had a problem I needed to deal with myself. Maybe I was a little sick and I ran these things down to her as best I could. I don't know if she understood. She always tried to take me for what I was. And I didn't want her to think I was any kind of great . . . she doesn't understand. She just turns off to narcotics. She doesn't want me to be around them or to have anything to do with them.

As these comments suggest, children are not so ignorant of the drug involvement as their mothers suppose. Moreover, they often serve as mirrors in which mothers may see a reflection of themselves. Perhaps out of curiosity, out of total innocence, or out of a childlike way to be helpful, children reflect the reality of adult behavior right back on them. One mother commented on her daughter's sincere efforts to help her "get well":

> And I can remember one time; she couldn't have been more than three or four. I was in bed. I didn't have any pills. She heard me on the phone trying to call this one and that one. I had prescriptions all over town. She found baby aspirin and brought it to me. She said to me, "Here mommie, here's your pills so you'll feel better." I felt awful.

Another mother described her child's protectiveness as follows:

> One day we were in the car and I was going to cash a check and she said, "Look out mommie, there's a policeman." It really startled me. I said, "What are you talking about?" And she said simply, "Lookie mommie, there's a policeman." She had heard me talking about it.

Still another mother told of how her 17-year-old daughter made her realize the choices she had to make:

> When I was released the first time, I had to say to myself, what is more important to me—my child and my life or my drugs? And now, you know, when I got out of here the first time, I was strung out on drugs. . . . When I first got out, my daughter had been living with her father. I said I wanted her back and he said no, so she ran away.

We lived together and we made it until I went back to jail. I stayed off drugs for eight months. And then I came back here. And when I got here I was down and depressed and I figured I needed them. She came up here for one time and she saw me high and she said, "You're back on them," and I had to pull myself up again. She has had a big impact on me.

These comments suggest that though inmate-mothers often try diligently to hide their drug involvement, their children usually detect and react to it. The children's reactions depend at least partially on their age. Younger children seemed to react protectively towards their mothers; older children and teenagers seemed to confront their mothers more directly. In any case, children's reactions heighten mothers' feelings of guilt and shame and in some ways make their schizophrenic lifestyle more difficult to maintain.

Mothers on Drugs: Parents, Siblings, or Friends?

Another common theme among inmate-mothers who had been involved with drugs on the outside was that they said their children often viewed them as siblings or as friends rather than as parents. [3] This theme most frequently occurred among inmate-mothers who had given birth to their first child early in life and had asked their own parents to raise the child either because of their youth or their lifestyle. Since the child's primary caregiver before prison was someone other than the natural mother, it is not surprising that the children did not perceive the natural mother as a parent in the traditional sense. One mother, whose son had been raised for two of his three years of life by his maternal grandmother, put it rather plainly: "I think he really knows I am his mother because I think a child always has this feeling anyway. He kind of feels like I am his sister too. I guess he should."

Another drug-addicted mother had turned over custody to her own mother unknowingly at the child's birth. Consequently, the child thought her natural mother was her sister:

I don't think my mother tells her anything about me. When she is going to bring [my daughter] to see me, she says, "Want to go see [inmate's name] tomorrow?" She thinks I am her sister because one day somebody asked her if she had any brothers and sisters and she said yes. I wasn't thinking and said, "No you don't." And she said, "Yes, I do." And I asked, "What's your brother's name?" And she said, "[male name]." Well, that's my brother and my mom agrees with her.

Despite the lack of a traditional filial relationship, some inmate-mothers reached across the span of years to their children in a different way. In need of someone to understand the idiosyncrasies of their lifestyle and in trying to ensure that the jigsaw pieces fit together in some coherent fashion for their children, some mothers regarded their children almost as equals. They often described their children as independent, mature beyond their years, and most of all, understanding of the drug problem. One mother noted the concern expressed by her 5-year-old daughter about her drug dealing: "She was about five at the time. One time she told me, 'I hope you ain't selling dope no more.' And then I knew she understood and I told her that I probably would not sell dope any more and I never did."

Another inmate-mother commented on the wisdom her young daughter displayed:

> She asked me, "When are you going to be home this time Pal?" She calls me Pal. She would also say, "When are you going to stop doing this? I told you not to do this. When are you going to listen? When are you going to stop getting into trouble?" That's why I hate to call her because that's the first thing she will say when I first get locked up. She'll say, "You see, I told you so." She's a smart little girl. She is too smart. It is like she got ESP or something because she will always tell me in advance. Then she will set back and smile real cute and say, "See, Pal, I told you so." And nine times out of ten she's usually right.

Frequently, inmate-mothers would go further in attributing maturity to their children. In some relationships there seemed to be a role reversal such that the child acted more the part of the parent and visa versa. For instance, one White mother of a 9-year-old girl said of her relationship with her daughter:

> It was like she was my mother and not me her mother. I would go to the store and she would say, "Will you be all right? I better go with you." She was just afraid of me leaving again. She was always watching out after me. Do this and do that. . . . In a way I depend on her a lot more than she depends on me. It's funny. It is like she is a lot more grown up than I ever was.

Similarly, these candid comments of a 46-year-old alcoholic mother about her relationship with her 15-year-old daughter further illustrate the role reversal and tremendous dependence upon the child for support and guidance:

> I lived together with my daughter before prison. I supported her OK. When I wasn't drinking, it was no problem. I am an alcoholic and managing money is a problem. If I hadn't boozed it away there would have been no problem. When I got into the dishonest way to get my money we managed to get by but my drinking habits made it so I couldn't afford to do anything. . . . She was not aware of my doing what I was doing but she was concerned because she knew I was hiding the booze—I kept it hid in the cupboards. I thought she didn't know but she did. The first time she saw me she knew I had drank. I thought I was hiding it in the bottle of coke. She said, "Mom, I knew you were coming back. Long before you ever went back." I asked her how she knew and she

said she knew because she knew that I was drinking and if I was drinking then it would just snowball as it has in the past.

The first time I came here I had a difficult time explaining to her. I was very ashamed of what was happening. We both cried a lot and I said that I had been arrested and would be going to court and that there was a possibility that they would put me in jail for awhile. She asked me what I did and it took probably an hour to try to tell her. She is a very adult young lady for eleven years old and she finally said, "Mom, just tell me what it was." She thought it was over cards because she knew that I had been playing a lot.

I worked very hard for the eleven months I was out on personal recognizance. I got my life under control. I quit drinking for the whole period of time. I was just working. . . . I mean I really turned over a whole bunch of new leaves. I just didn't want her to see me crumble. . . . We are very close. In fact, it's almost a role reversal where . . . I am dependent on her love. I make very few decisions without consulting her . . . . I have allowed myself to be that dependent.

I feel very guilty about being back here. I've been here once. I knew what I was doing was wrong. . . . I feel very guilty that I ever went back to that first drink. I thought I took all those pretty courses at the prison and I know my inner thoughts and I can handle anything. I manipulate myself and everybody around me. I can't handle it. I manipulate everybody around me to allow me to have another drink.

Summary

Just as other drug users, inmate-mothers admittedly take drugs to mask problems, conceal plaguing concerns, or avoid a sterile existence. Perhaps they expect the magic of drugs to transform their everyday world into something more. Some start out at an early age experimenting with peers to use or sell drugs. Others become "pharmaceutical junkies," as one mother put it, as adults. For those who subsequently become parents, the demands of a drug habit ultimately collide with the demands of children. Therefore, over and above the shame they feel because of their crime, conviction, and separation due to incarceration, these mothers have an additional burden of guilt to bear. The inevitable conflict resulting from these incompatible demands leads to what herein has been called a schizophrenic lifestyle—junkie by day and mother by night or vice versa. Whether or not this lifestyle could have been sustained had these mothers not been imprisoned is a question worthy of careful examination in future research.

However, for most of the mothers who ended up in prison, their previous life patterns generated an intensive guilt about their drug habits as well as about their crimes. Inmate-mothers who had been prostitutes on the outside had still another complicating factor. To the pills and diapers is added the fast pace of street life, which often precluded developing a closeness with children even from birth. For some mothers, the physical and mental dependence upon drugs created a dependence on their children for support and guidance. This role reversal, operating perhaps imperceptibly at first, seemed to play a large part in shaping the relationships between some inmate-mothers and their children.

For all these mothers, if nothing else, incarceration provides a time out, a chance to think about their past behaviors and the effects on them and their families. One mother said:

> If you can't see them, they probably think that if you loved them, you would not have done the things you did. When I think about it now that I am completely off of drugs, I wonder why I did it. At the time I did it, it seemed like the thing to do. She needed things and I needed things and I didn't have any money. I couldn't stand to see anybody wanting for something so I just went and wrote a check and got what everybody needed plus more.

Another mother mused:

> I know I have neglected her a lot and it just wasn't me. And now that I am not doing drugs it all comes back and I think about it a lot. In a way I feel like this is what it took to even help me. I might have been worse. I want to build up our relationship.

A Black 21-year-old mother, of a 4-year-old boy, who had become very involved in prison activities said that she wanted to turn herself around upon release:

> You know, since I have been here, I have had time to think about my child, my family, how my parents feel about me and I really don't think I am going to get back off into drugs. I am just going to get a complete new environment. . . . I just don't want any more to do with drugs because I know it will have effects on my son and on me and I will probably be back here again and he will be at the age where he will realize what is going on and I don't want him to know anything about that.

Inmate-mothers who sold or used drugs on the outside, no less than nondrug users, care for and want their children back upon release. For these women, however, an additional problem is how to deal with the drug problem and with their children on the outside. Ideally, kicking the habit for good is the solution. Realistically, how many inmate-mothers will do this? For these women there are other questions as well: Is it realistic to try to hide a habit from a teenager who may be on the brink of experimentation? Will hiding a habit enhance the relationship with a child or one's own self-esteem? Finally, does drug-taking behavior necessarily mean that these mothers should relinquish the rights to their children because they have been—possibly will be —junkies? There are no simple answers to these questions.

What is needed is a greater understanding of the conditions that lead to use of drugs, the way in which inmate-mothers—or any mothers—may learn to control their habit. Most importantly, mothers need to understand the impacts of their involvement with drugs on their relationship with children before they end up in prison. For those who are already imprisoned, programs designed to enhance mother-child bonds during incarceration could go a long way towards generating this kind of understanding.

Notes

1. Prior literature indicated that prostitution is a means of support for female addicts. In this sense, female addicts have been depicted as prostitutes. However, more recent research has challenged this notion. Studies of female addicts and prostitutes have found that addicts may or may not be prostitutes and may or may not have been arrested for crimes (File et al. 1974; James et al. 1979; Inciardi 1980). The present study suggests that of the 55 inmate-mothers who indicated during the taped interviews that they had been involved with narcotic or nonnarcotic drugs prior to their current incarceration, only 11 had been involved in prostitution to support themselves. Whether or not prostitution served as a primary means of support for their drug habit is unclear from the data. Only 4 of the women discussed prostitution as a significant source of support at any time in their lives. More often, inmate-mothers reported that they had engaged in property crimes such as shoplifting as a means of supporting their drug habit. Other studies of female criminality and drugs have also noted that property offenses are predominant among women with a drug history (Miller 1980; Inciardi 1980).
2. Henriques (1981) found in a study of 30 inmate-mothers in a northeastern prison that 16 (53 percent) reportedly had used drugs and 14 (47 percent) had not. However, the focus of the study did not include an analysis of the impacts of drug use on the mother's self-perceptions or on the mother-child relationship (Henriques 1981:57).
3. It may be that the children's perceptions of sibling relationships, role reversals with children, and dependence upon them for support and guidance was more a function of the inmate-mother's emotional development, personality traits, or other characteristics which led to drug-taking rather than a correlate of the drug-taking itself. The extent to which many of these points may be accurate remains to be examined in future research on relationships between inmate-mothers and children. What is needed is a systematic study of the relationships and social networks of mothers who use or sell drugs including a subset of those who are arrested, convicted, and imprisoned. Perhaps the points raised herein will be a stimulus to this broader research.

7

Programs to Strengthen Ties

In this country, inmate-mothers usually maintain ties with children through letters, phone calls, and intermittent brief visits. In recent years, however, there have been scattered efforts to encourage the development and strengthening of mother-child bonds on a continuing basis. The programs to strengthen mother-child bonds in prisons may be divided into three categories: nurseries for newborn babies, extended visiting programs, and child development and/or parenting programs.[1]

Children born to women in prison usually leave the hospital with another caretaker within a few days after birth. Nurseries, however, enable inmate-mothers to leave together with their children and to spend the first few weeks and months developing an all-important mother-child bond. In a nursery setting, inmate-mothers may engage in maternal activities, such as breast feeding, which would otherwise be impossible. Since most women in prison want to care for their children after release, the chance to develop a close relationship at birth sets the stage for subsequent involvement. Feeding, diapering, and caring for their own newborn babies may instill warmth, love, and a sense of responsibility within inmate-mothers.

Currently, the only nursery operational within a prison in this country is at the Women's Correctional Institution at Bedford Hills, New York. The nursery, which has been part of the institution since it opened, is located on the top floor of a building on the prison grounds. Women move into the nursery within the last few months of their pregnancy, give birth in a hospital near the institution, and then live in the nursery in a wing next to the babies. Mothers may stay up to a year in the nursery where their primary responsibility is the care of their infants.

More recently, the Federal Bureau of Prisons developed a similar kind of program outside the prison walls. In 1978, the Shared Beginnings Program was created as a joint project of the Bureau of Prisons and the Emergency Shelter Program in Hayward, California. The program moved to Brandon House in San Jose, California, in October of that year. Eligible federal prisoners may move into the house in the seventh month of their pregnancy and remain there with their newborn infants for up to four months (Shared Beginnings 1980).

Another program for mothers in the Federal Correctional Institution at Pleasanton is Prison Match: The Pleasanton Children's Center Program. Begun in 1978 with financial assistance from private foundations, the program is designed to strengthen bonds between inmate-mothers and children, teach inmate-mothers parenting skills and prepare them for careers in early childhood education. In addition, the program reaches out into the community to generate positive community attitudes and assist correctional administrators in preparing policies and planning programs that take into account the special needs of inmate-mothers. The community has learned about issues faced by inmate-mothers through an extensive media campaign and commentaries prepared for television. Program staff have worked with the California State Bar Association to improve legal statutes that apply to inmate-mothers and their children. Moreover, they have been instrumental in assisting other correctional agencies, such as the San Francisco and Alameda County Sheriff's Departments and the California Institution for Women, in planning similar types of programs (National Council on Crime and Delinquency [undated]:7–8).

In Massachusetts, a program called Aid to Incarcerated Mothers (AIM), jointly sponsored by the Urban Planning Aid office in Boston and the Family Project at the Massachusetts Correctional Institution for Women at Framingham, was begun to provide inmate-mothers serving a year or more with an individual volunteer who acts as an advocate to help facilitate visiting, deal with agencies at the mother's request, and others who may affect her child's life. The thrust of the program is to give inmate-mothers information about resources to enable her to make realistic decisions about her child both during and following incarceration (Thomases 1982:1, 3).

Some institutions enable inmate-mothers to visit with children on days and times other than the regularly scheduled visiting hours. Extended visits may last a half or full day or may continue overnight or throughout the weekend. These kinds of programs give mothers and children a chance to interact with one another in a more relaxed manner for a longer period. A number of institutions have also begun child development or parenting programs to assist inmate-mothers in learning to understand their children and possible problems they may confront in resuming parental responsibilities after release.

At the time of the study, seven states and the federal system had developed programs that incorporate one or more of these types of programs to strengthen mother-child bonds during incarceration.[2] This chapter describes the institutions and the programs developed to retain ties at the Daniel Boone Career Development Center (DBCDC) in Kentucky and the Purdy Treatment Center for Women (PTC) in Washington state.

Daniel Boone Career Development Center (DBCDC)

Overview of the Institution

The DBCDC was opened in August 1976 with a Law Enforcement Assistance Administration grant from the state criminal justice planning agency. The prison was opened to alleviate overcrowding at the Kentucky Correctional Institution for Women (KCIW). The "Goals and Performance Objectives of the Kentucky Bureau of Corrections" issued in September 1976 identified the establishment of a minimum security institution for women as a priority for the Kentucky Bureau of Corrections. The rationale for this effort was to separate young first offenders from multiple or repeat offenders and to provide a community-based environment in which these women could receive more individualized programming to assist their reintegration into society as productive members (Daniel Boone Career Development Center 1978:H2).

Located in Belleview, Kentucky, the center was situated on a twelve-acre tract along the Ohio River in rural Boone County. The physical plant was composed of eight major buildings which were leased from the federal government. Directly adjacent to the institution were several residences which comprise Belleview, Kentucky. To this extent, the institution was located directly within a community.

The philosophy of the institution echoed the rationale for its creation: "The primary goal is to release strong, independent, and responsible women into the community, [to prepare women to] cope with the high level of responsibility" required by the community (Daniel Boone Career Development Center 1979:2). To this end, the programmatic orientation of the institution included on-grounds activities such as G.E.D. and living skills training and several off-grounds activities such as college, vocational training, volunteer participation in a weekly tutoring program for junior and senior high school students, and working with children in a group home in nearby Burlington, Kentucky. In addition, women could participate in arts and crafts, an exercise class, and other recreational activities on grounds. Off-grounds activities included shopping trips, going out for pizza or movies. Women could carry up to $15 on campus to purchase candy, pop, or cigarettes. For off-grounds shopping trips women could take larger sums of money to purchase clothes, food, etc. However, anything in excess of $15 which was not spent had to be returned to the residents' accounts. When requested, women were required to provide receipts of purchases made.

Between 1976 and 1979, there were two superintendents. The second superintendent implemented a "performance based incentive system" called the Level System (Daniel Boone Career Development Center 1979:21). This behavior modification approach described to residents what behaviors were expected in order to earn and retain various privileges at each level. There were three levels—the higher the level, the greater the privileges. At intake, a resident's placement was determined by her level at the Kentucky Correctional Institution for Women. Residents on levels 1 or 2 at KCIW were placed on level 1 at DBCDC. Those on level 3 were placed on level 2 and those on levels 4 or 5 were placed on level 3. At DBCDC the lowest level activities were more restricted to campus although residents would participate in one off-grounds shopping trip each month. At higher levels, residents earned more frequent and more varied off-grounds privileges. There was a minimum time limit of 30 days on level 1 but no formal time limits for other levels. The Classification Committee, which met monthly, reviewed each resident's progress and decided her current placement.

Mother Offspring Life Development (MOLD) Program and Systematic Training for Effective Parenting (STEP)

Development and Operations. Against this backdrop, the Mother Offspring Life Development Program (MOLD) was begun in November 1977. The program began as the result of the efforts of DBCDC's former nurse, who first heard about the concept at a Kentucky Council on Crime and Delinquency conference where Ms. Jacqueline Crawford, then superintendent of the Nebraska Center for Women, presented a paper about the MOLD project operative in her institution. The nurse enthusiastically reported the information to DBCDC's superintendent and they worked together to develop and implement the program. The concept of enabling residents and children to develop closer ties and to assist residents in relating to their children in a positive way fit in with the institution's overall philosophy of fostering a sense of responsibility among residents.

According to staff and administrators who were at DBCDC at the time of the program's inception, there were no major obstacles encountered in developing and implementing the MOLD program. The first MOLD weekend was held in November 1977. Shortly thereafter both the nurse and superintendent left the center. The succeeding superintendent endorsed the concept and asked a correctional officer to coordinate the program; she was responsible for the program at the time of the study. The purpose of the program was to "enable the parent and child to interact constructively in a setting which would enable both to become better acquainted." Within this framework, major objectives of the program included: placing responsibility for child care on the mother; enabling mother and child to form closer bonds and feel part of one another's lives; minimizing stereotypes of "mother in prison" for children; and facilitating the child's understanding of his/her mother's current living situation (Beasley [undated]:1).

Theoretically, MOLD weekends were held once each month. Early the week before, women requested to have their children come to the institution.

Each woman contacted the child's caretaker and arranged for transportation to and from the institution. In addition, she signed a liability waiver which indicated that in the event the child was injured at the institution the responsibility rested with her. To date, however, none of the children who have participated in MOLD weekends have been injured.

The eligibility requirements for mothers were that they be on level 2 and that they participated in the Systematic Training for Effective Parenting Program. The first requirement suggests that having children at the institution for the weekend is a privilege women must earn. Children had to be up to age 15 for girls and up to age 12 for boys and free of illnesses. Because of space limitations, usually only 2 children per woman were allowed to visit on any one weekend; however, at the time of the study, this rule had not been enforced.

Children arrived late Friday afternoon and stayed until Sunday afternoon. Wherever women were allowed on campus, children were also allowed. Mothers were required to be responsible for the supervision of their children at all times. Activities during the weekend were relatively unstructured in order to maximize the time mothers and children would spend together doing what they wished. However, some scheduled activities did occur. For instance, sometimes women and children took off-campus shopping trips. In addition, other residents served as volunteers to supervise arts and crafts activities on Saturday mornings or storytelling for the children, in order to give mothers some free time. Since the women ate in their own cottages on weekends, meals were shared with cottage residents. Women paid for the children's meals, 15¢ for breakfast, 30¢ for lunch and 20¢ for supper. Money collected for the meals went to the purchase of arts and crafts materials for the weekend. In addition, mothers could purchase food from the local store to prepare for their children.

As the MOLD program got underway, staff reported that the women expressed a need to understand and to learn ways to handle discipline with children during the MOLD weekends. Based upon this need, an additional element, Systematic Training for Effective Parenting (STEP), was incorporated into the MOLD program in November 1978. At the time of the study, the two elements of the program operated in conjunction with one another. That is, a resident had to be enrolled in STEP before she could have her children visit on the MOLD weekends. The primary purpose of the STEP program was to assist women in skill acquisition as parents by learning to understand and communicate with children as people. Weekly evening meetings were held to discuss communications skills, handling discipline, and other topics related to parenting.

Skills acquired during weekly discussions in STEP would hopefully be practiced during MOLD weekends and perhaps carried over into handling children's behavior after release. However, given the multiplicity of factors which combine to influence behavior following release, this long-range benefit may be tenuous at best. In any event, there has been no documentation of postrelease effectiveness of the MOLD or STEP programs in assisting ex-offenders to reestablish positive relationships with their children.

Frequency of MOLD Weekends. In the first 20 months of operation of the MOLD program (from November 1977 through June 1979), a total of 41 mothers and 59 children or an average of 2.1 mothers and 3.0 children participated per month. The average daily population at DBCDC for this period was roughly 31 women per month.[3] Thus, about 7 percent of the population had been involved in the MOLD program each month since its inception.

This small percentage of the total population may be accounted for by at least two factors. As will be discussed more fully later, the lack of transportation or distance from children's placements limited participation, and during winter months hazardous driving conditions inhibited travel even for regular visits. Also, for two months, a nurse was not present for the weekends. One requirement for MOLD weekends was that a nurse be available for 24 hours. Without a nurse from mid-April to mid-May, MOLD weekends were not held. Thus because of hazardous winter driving and lack of a nurse between February and June 1979, no MOLD weekends were held. Table 7.1 shows the frequency of MOLD weekends from the program's inception through June 1979.

Staff and Residents Perceptions of and Reactions to the MOLD and STEP Programs. At the time of the study there were 28 residents and 19 staff at the institution. Eight (42 percent) staff and 26 (93 percent) residents were

TABLE 7.1
Frequency of MOLD Weekends, November 1977–June 1979

Time Frame	Months for MOLD	Number of Mothers	Number of Children
11/77 to 9/78[1]	N/A	35	51
10/78 to 12/78[2]	12/78	4	6
1/79 to 3/79[3]	1/79	2	2
4/79 to 6/79[4]	N/A	N/A	N/A
Total		41	59

Source: DBCDC Final Progress Report, Undated, p. 3.
Source: DBCDC Quarterly Performance Report, December 31, 1978.
Source: DBCDC Quarterly Performance Report, March 31, 1979 p. 3.
Source: DBCDC Quarterly Performance Report, June 30, 1979 p. 3.

interviewed. Staff members included 2 administrators and 7 staff who worked most closely with residents as counselors or teachers. Two residents were unavailable at the time of the study: one was on furlough and the other had suffered a heart attack.[4]

With respect to participation in the MOLD programs, only 3 mothers had had their children at the institution for the MOLD weekend. Two of these women had had their children more than once and one had discontinued participation as transportation became a problem. For 8 of the mothers, the primary reason for the lack of participation was that since their admission there had been no MOLD weekends. Four of the women had been admitted in December 1978. Between that time and the time of the interviews in April 1979, there had been but one MOLD weekend, in January 1979. As noted previously, participation in the MOLD program required level 2 status. Since it took a month to reach this level, these women reported that at the time the weekend was held they were not yet eligible for participation. Table 7.2 presents the number of women who had been involved in MOLD at the time of the interviews.

Four of the mothers, admitted since December 1978, expressed an interest in participation when MOLD weekends resumed. The other 4 also expressed an interest but said that transportation or distance from the child's placement would preclude their involvement. These reasons for lack of involvement

TABLE 7.2
Residents' Involvement in MOLD at Time of the Study

Involvement	%	N
Yes:	11	(3)
No:		
Weekends not held since arrival	29	(8)
Transportation	7	(2)
Children older than upper-age limits	14	(4)
No Children	32	(9)
Subtotal	82	(23)
Don't know/not interviewed	7	(2)
Total	100	(28)

were common among older women. Both staff and residents generally supported the program. The most common reason given by staff in support of the program was that it enabled women and children to interact for an extended period and to share daily routine experiences such as meals or bedtime. Among residents, the most common reason was that they enjoyed being with children. One nonmother who had experienced a MOLD weekend noted:

> You get to feel good inside because you're doing things with the kids. I don't have kids but having the other ones up here reminds me of my own large family back home. There aren't hassles with discipline or anything like that. Sure sometimes the kids don't mind or the mothers don't make them mind but it isn't that often. The kids don't fight with one another and the mothers don't either.

Another common reason for support of the program was that it alleviated children's fears and provided them with a realistic perspective of the mother's current living situation. One mother said:

> The program's good 'cause it keeps mothers in touch with their children. It lets kids know where their mother is and how she's living. TV makes prison look big and ugly. But this place doesn't look like that and the kids can see for themselves what it's really like and not worry about their mother.

Despite general supportiveness, both staff and residents expressed some reservations about the MOLD program. Perhaps the most significant problem cited by both staff and residents was the lack of transportation for children to and from the institution. Mothers were required to arrange for transportation by themselves. However, most of the residents were from the Louisville metropolitan area, some 200 miles south of the DBCDC. Transportation to bring children on Friday afternoon and again to take them home on Sunday afternoon was often difficult to arrange. Seven of the women said that even when MOLD weekends resumed they would be unable to arrange for transporation. As one mother put it: "I can't get my babies up here and it's painful to be around other children. The way transportation is I don't much care for the program, but I would like it better if I could get my own children up here." Another mother had not seen her children even during regular visiting hours since her arrival at DBCDC because the distance was so great. As it was impossible to have the children visit at all, she defensively rejected the program as unnecessary: "My kids live with my parents. They can't get here 'cause it's too far away. I don't need the program 'cause I already have a close understanding with my kids. I'd get upset when they'd leave after the weekend anyway, so I don't want them to stay." A second problem cited by staff and residents was housing. Some staff and residents felt that a separate housing area was needed for mothers and children during MOLD weekends. Two women, both nonmothers, expressed concern about the lack of privacy when children were present. One nonmother commented: "I have been here for two MOLD weekends and it nearly drove me bats. There aren't any problems with discipline or anything like that. It's just that I'm not into kids. . . . It's not bad to have kids up once a month but that's enough." The other nonmother had not yet experienced a MOLD weekend but thought it would be too noisy having children around constantly unless mothers and children were assigned to one cottage.

In conjunction with this problem, some staff said that sometimes children were not supervised closely enough by mothers during the MOLD weekends. This could cause some disruption for other residents. For example, during one weekend, a resident's sweater was cut up with scissors by an unsupervised child. However, staff also pointed out that these incidents have occurred only rarely and that residents handled this situation fairly: an agreement was made to replace the sweater, but the resident who owned the sweater said it was unnecessary.

Staff indicated that they felt more responsible for the children's safety when mothers' supervision lapsed, especially since the Ohio River bordered the institution. However, there were no major incidents or mishaps involving children during the MOLD weekends. There was a small amount of play equipment and toys for young children. Staff suggested purchasing additional equipment but noted that this entailed reordering priorities in budgeting.

An additional problem mothers mentioned was the painfulness in saying good-bye at the end of the weekend, but the problem diminished as children came more often. One mother remarked: "The hardest part is saying good-bye. But you know, P.J., it gets easier each time 'cause you know they're coming back and you're getting closer to leaving." At the time of the study, five of the mothers were attending STEP classes. Two others had dropped them, one because she felt the classes had not been helpful and the other because the child was no longer able to participate in MOLD weekends. The primary reason given for involvement in STEP was that it was required in order to have children come for MOLD weekends. Three of the mothers involved also said that they were learning to better understand their children. One woman said, "It helps me in disciplining and understanding children and in knowing how to talk to them after four years apart."

Some staff contended that there was a lack of continuity between the STEP and MOLD programs. Conceptually, the STEP program discussed the dynamics of parenting skills, and the MOLD weekend served as a means to implement and test skills acquired. However, with only one MOLD weekend each month, it was difficult to put into practice all the skills learned at each STEP meeting. Moreover, activities during the MOLD weekends were not structured specifically to test particular parenting skills. Therefore, behaviors related to concepts discussed in STEP meetings might not surface during the MOLD weekends.

As noted previously, since the program began MOLD weekends had not been scheduled regularly. This lack of consistency in scheduling made it difficult for mothers to test out the skills they had learned in STEP. Moreover, relationships between mothers and children which may have been reinforced during previous MOLD weekends might need to be redeveloped. The number of times a mother had been able to see her child for MOLD weekends had been minimal for two reasons: the lack of transportation and distance from the child's placement to the institution and the average length of stay for residents at DBCDC being only about 6.5 months (Daniel Boone Career Development Center [undated]:6). Given the lack of consistency in scheduling MOLD weekends, most mothers might see their children only once or twice during their incarceration at the DBCDC. Some staff felt that this was insufficient time to reaffirm relationships or to work out significant problem areas between residents and children. For this reason they suggested scheduling MOLD weekends more regularly, once every month.

Some staff raised concerns over the possible impact of the MOLD experience on the children. On one hand, the experience of sharing the weekend with the mother might benefit the relationship. On the other hand, what kinds of feelings did the children have about their mothers and themselves when they left, or what possible impact might the experience have on the children's lives or their relationships with their current caretakers? To date no one has explored the impact of participation in MOLD on the children.

A few staff indicated that they would like to know more about the MOLD and STEP programs in order to be more supportive of them. As one staff member remarked: "We all have input into the growth and development of the residents. I could provide more positive input to help if I knew more about the content and nature of the programs." Despite reservations expressed about the MOLD and STEP programs, all the staff and twenty-two of the residents interviewed expressed support for the programs. These results suggest that at least half of the staff and most residents in this institution endorsed the concept of having children stay overnight with mothers. The problems mentioned point up potential areas for improvement. The three most important are: (1) providing transportation for children to the institution, (2) holding MOLD weekends regularly each month, and (3) providing more continuity between STEP and MOLD programs.

Continuation of the Mother-Child Programs Following Closing of the Daniel Boone Career Development Center

DBCDC was closed in the fall of 1981. Inmates were transferred to a minimum security unit at the Kentucky Correctional Institution for Women

(KCIW) outside the walls of the main compound. In this environment, women inmates currently have access to community facilities in the Louisville metropolitan area. In addition, the services and training (food services, recreation, nursing) from within the walls of KCIW are available to minimum security women.[5]

Shortly after the development of the MOLD program at DBCDC, a parenting program permitting ten full-day visits annually was instituted at KCIW through financial cooperation between the institution and the River City chapter of the Business and Professional Women (BPW). In the spring of 1983, the overnight component was added to that program. Additional staff required to deliver that program in a multisecurity environment have been provided again in conjunction with the volunteer community group. Thus, as of publication the program described by the present study remains intact. Program goals are essentially the same as are many of the problems described.

The purposes of the program are to strengthen parenting skills, to provide open, healthy, and extended visits between inmate-mothers and children, and to maintain mother-child bonds for the children's emotional health and for the mother's positive reentry into the family upon release. The program entails classroom instruction for mothers, Kid's Day on each of ten Saturdays throughout the year, and overnight visitation.

Overnights are held in the chapel, and full-day visits in the recreation area. Due to the multisecurity nature of the facility, participants are separated from the main body of the population. Both indoor and outdoor areas are available and movement is unrestricted within designated areas. Appropriate equipment for indoor and outdoor play activities have been purchased through volunteer community groups; meals for the children are paid for by the BPW.

To be eligible, inmates must have been a KCIW resident for at least thirty days, and must complete parenting classes. Unlike the former program at DBCDC, there is no need to be at a certain level. The levels system continues in use at KCIW but is currently under litigation through a class action suit brought in the fall of 1981. Ten mothers and 5 helpers, who may or may not be mothers, are selected for each overnight visit. Mothers may have one child per overnight visit and more than one child on Kid's Day.

Usually 15 to 25 women and an equal number of children participate on Kid's Day and fifteen women and ten children participate on the overnight visits. Children of either sex may be from age 10 through 15 and must be the mother's natural children. For Kid's Day, children arrive between 10:00 and 11:00 A.M. on Saturday and leave at 4:00 P.M. For the overnight visits, children arrive between 6:00 and 7:00 P.M. on Friday and leave at 4:00 P.M. on Saturday. Since the spring of 1983, when the overnight program began, twenty-five women have had a child stay overnight with them; as of 1 December 1983 fifteen of these women participated at least twice.

The Purdy Treatment Center for Women

Overview of the Institution

The Purdy Treatment Center for Women (PTC) was opened in February 1971 and is the only women's prison in Washington state. Located near Tacoma, on eighty acres of land, the institution physically resembles a well-landscaped community college. Within the perimeter of the main compound there are five housing units, an admissions and orientation unit for newly admitted residents, three units for the general population and a maximum security unit. Each unit houses thirty-two to thirty-six residents. The sewing rooms in each of the four main living units were converted into double rooms to accommodate an increasing population. Outside the main compound is an apartment complex consisting of eleven units which may house up to three restricted minimum custody women. The residents attend programs at the facilities. Work release inmates live off campus.

Women carry keys to their individual rooms and, within an allowable clothing inventory, wear their own clothes. In addition, there is some freedom of movement to various parts of the campus; however, residents must sign out of their living units to a designated area and for a specified purpose and time period. Newly admitted residents are required to complete 240 hours of work in the kitchen. Following completion of this requirement, residents program for at least 40 hours a week in selected activities. Among these activities are school, vocational classes, and counseling of various types (alcohol, drug, family).

Since it opened, PTC's orientation has included a focus on assisting mothers to maintain ties with their children. Conceptually, several assumptions underlie this approach. One basic premise has been that parenthood is a responsibility rather than a privilege. Although incarcerated and not totally responsible for her children, a mother has not relinquished her parental rights; she should be involved in decision making in matters which affect her children's lives as much as possible. A woman's identity is partially defined by her role as a mother, and planning for institutional programming should take this important role into account. Finally, children should know where their mothers are, and the conditions under which and why they are there. This information may assist them in adjusting more easily to their current placement and may lessen feelings that they have been abandoned (Buckles and Lafazia 1973:43–50).

Within this framework, various programs concerning child care and relationships with children have been developed. These programs include a child development course, a nursery school, special visits for children, and a foster-care placement program. Each of the first three of these programs will be discussed briefly. The foster-care placement program will be discussed in Chapter 8.[6]

Child Development

The child development course has been a part of the institution since it opened. The general objectives of this three-month course are to: increase awareness of the likenesses and differences in children, especially children of preschool ages; recognize that children normally develop at varying rates but in a fairly predictable pattern; and utilize knowledge in nursery school children's literature, music, and basic skills.

Topics covered in the course include intellectual growth; emotional, physical, and social development; sex education and health and safety. In addition, residents prepare arts and crafts and science and music projects. Each student is required to record observations of assigned children for each topic throughout the course (Chapman 1978a). When the course began, the residents worked with children in day care centers outside the institution. However, not all residents were eligible to leave the institution. This need for an on-site "laboratory" for the child development course was partially responsible for the creation of the nursery school.

Nursery School

Development and Operations. An informal survey of PTC residents in 1971 by the home economics and child development instructor revealed that 85 percent of the residents at that time had children and wanted to develop parenting skills. In addition, the survey indicated that residents felt inadequate as mothers and often threatened by children's caretakers: "The women gradually lose their self-image as successful or even adequate mothers . . . As a result their relationships with their children do not improve, nor is . . . self-esteem strengthened (Chapman 1978b)." Based upon these deficiencies, the home economics teacher and the principal of the PTC school initiated plans to develop the nursery school in 1972. During the two-year planning process, various problems in developing the nursery school were encountered. For one thing, physical aspects of the school building had to be modified to accommodate a bathroom for children and to provide an outside door from the nursery school to the fenced-in play area. Modifications of this nature in a prison are difficult to obtain and required clearance at several levels.

Approximately $19,500 in federal funds was finally secured in September 1974 through a Title I Elementary Secondary Education Act (ESEA) grant. Although residents were involved in planning the school itself, they assisted in ordering some $4,000 worth of play equipment and toys, in assembling furniture, and in decorating the school room. Publicity for the program was initially handled by advertisements in local newspapers. The response was so good that this method was discontinued shortly after the school opened and additional students have since been recruited by word of mouth. An experienced nursery school teacher was hired and the program was opened in October 1975. The school became known as "Pooh's Corner" because of the brightly colored story-book characters painted on one wall.

The major objectives of the school, which have changed little since the program began, are to provide residents an opportunity to work with and increase an understanding of preschool children other than their own; increase basic communications skills by teaching children; and enable residents to accumulate up to ninety hours of work experience in a nursery school setting that may be useful in obtaining jobs relating to day care upon release (Chapman 1978b:1–2).

The school serves up to 24 students ranging in age from 3 to 5 years old. Children are recruited on a first come first served basis from communities immediately surrounding the institution. There is no cost to parents to send children to the school other than a $2 liability charge for insurance. Children attend the school two days a week either on Monday and Wednesday or Tuesday and Thursday from 9:00 A.M. to 11:30 A.M. Originally Friday was left open for residents to work with their own children in the nursery. However, residents were unable to arrange transportation for their children to the institution, so this aspect of the program was discontinued.

In order to be eligible for the program, residents must first complete the child development course. Next, a screening process considers the woman's "attitude, social and emotional behaviors, and the type of crime" (Chapman 1978b:3). Women convicted of child-related offenses are not eligible for participation. In the past, final selection has been made by the child development instructor in consultation with the nursery school teacher.[7] Residents usually work in the school two mornings a week. There are thus aides working with the teacher in the classroom each day. The aides assist in preparing snacks and materials, teaching songs and games, supervising play activities, and handling discipline.

Since the nursery school opened, there have been two teachers. A major goal of the current teacher, hired in 1977, is to teach women alternative ways of handling discipline by modeling appropriate behaviors. For example, instead of saying no to a child she emphasizes what the child can do. She views the program as a means of providing women with some insight into their own as well as into the children's behavior. From her perspective, positive interactions with children enhance a resident's perceptions of her abilities to deal with others effectively. She may then feel better about herself.[8]

Staff working closely with the program noted that there have been relatively few problems in the program's operations. Perhaps the greatest difficulty has resulted from a change in departmental policy regarding outings for medium custody residents. Prior to mid-1978, residents classified as medium custody were allowed to go on special escorted outings away from the institution. Aides in the nursery school program accompanied the class and children's parents on picnics, nature hikes, and other field trips. In addition to providing the children with new experiences, these trips enabled residents to relate to the children in new settings and to interact with parents informally in unstructured activities. The trips further provided parents a chance to observe the relationships developed between their children and the residents. According to the nursery school teacher, everyone worked together to prepare meals or clean up picnic sites and the experiences were always enjoyable. Moreover, there have never been any bad incidents involving residents, parents, or children on any of the outings. In fact, she noted that residents were very protective towards the children and carefully made sure that all the children were accounted for when it was time to leave.

In mid-1978, a new departmental policy was issued which precluded medium security residents from participating in off-campus outings. This policy has made it difficult to take nursery school children on field trips. The teacher needs adult assistance in supervising children away from campus. According to the policy, only residents classified as minimum custody are now allowed to participate in off-campus outings. Most of the residents participating in the nursery school program, however, are medium custody and therefore ineligible to go on field trips. Thus, most aides can no longer share in the off-grounds experiences with children which were a valuable part of the program in the past.

Extent of Resident Involvement in the Nursery School. Since the program began, 47 residents have been involved as aides in the program. During the first four years of operation 13 (8 percent), 16 (9 percent), 10 (5 percent), and 8 (4 percent) women respectively were involved as aides. These percentages were determined by dividing the number of women involved during each school year by the average daily population for the months during which the nursery school was in operation (Table 7.3). Of those enrolled, 43 percent (20) completed the ninety-hour program and received certificates. The remaining 57 percent (27) did not complete the program (Table 7.4).

Information regarding why residents had not completed the program was available only for women enrolled since 1977. Of these 18 residents, 14 had not completed the program. Of these 14 women, 5 (36 percent) had been transferred to the minimum security unit outside the main campus. Once a resident leaves the main course, she no longer participates in programs on campus. Another 5 (36 percent) residents had terminated their participation though the reasons for their termination were unclear. The remaining 4 (28

TABLE 7.3
Percentage of PTC Residents Involved in the Nursery School 1975–1979, by School Year

School Year (Sept. – June)	Average Daily Population for School Year [1]	Residents Involved	Residents Involved %
1975–76	155.3	13	8
1976–77	182.9	16	9
1977–78	193.8	10	5
1978–79	194.7	8	4

1. These figures were obtained from the PTC Records Office.

percent) women had completed the school year but had been transferred out of the institution during summer recess before they had completed the ninety-hour program (Table 7.5).

Residents Perceptions of the Child Development and Nursery School Programs. During the interview, residents were asked whether or not they had participated in any of the programs designed to assist them in understanding or relating to children. Fifty-one (50 percent) of the women interviewed[9] said that they had been involved in at least one program of this nature. The remaining 50 (50 percent) said that they had not been involved. Of the women involved, 19 (37 percent) had participated in some type of group counseling relating to understanding children or feelings about the separation from children; 18 (35 percent) had been involved in the child development class; 7 (14 percent) had sought individual counseling as it relates to parenting, and 5 (10 percent) had served as aides in the nursery school.[10]

Women who were not involved in the programs gave one or more reasons. Women without children saw no need for participation. Some mothers felt confident that they could raise their children upon release without these classes. Mothers with older children felt the programs were geared to younger children and did not provide material relevant to the ages of their children. Other women had other priorities they wished to pursue such as vocational training. A few mothers expressed interest but said that they had not been involved at the institution long enough to know what types of programs were available (Table 7.6).

Five of the women interviewed, all mothers, had served as nursery school aides. All of these residents considered the nursery school experience valuable in understanding children's behavior. In addition, they uniformly said that it provided a refreshing change from the routine of prison life and enabled them to interact positively with others. One resident said, "There are a lot of games here. But in the nursery school you can be yourself. You can play with the kids and watch them learn. I just love kids anyway." Women involved with

TABLE 7.4
Residents' Involvement in the PTC Nursery School, 1975–1979

Program Involvement	1975–76		1976–77		1977–78		1978–79		Total	
	%	N	%	N	%	N	%	N	%	N
Completed program	62	(8)	50	(8)	20	(2)	25	(2)	43	(20)
Did not complete program	38	(5)	50	(8)	80	(8)	75	(6)	57	(27)
Total	100	(13)	100	(16)	100	(10)	100	(8)	100	(47)

Source: Attendance records of residents for Purdy Treatment Center Nursery School, 1975–79.

TABLE 7.5
Reasons for Noncompletion of the Nursery School Program, 1977–1979

Reason	1977-78[1]		1978-79		Total	
	%	N	%	N	%	N
Transferred from institution during school year	37	(3)	33	(2)	36	(5)
Dropped program	37	(3)	33	(2)	36	(5)
Transferred from institution at end of school year	25	(2)	33	(2)	28	(4)
Total	99	(8)	99	(6)	100	(14)

Source: Attendance records of residents for Purdy Treatment Center Nursery School, 1975–79.
1. Percentages may not equal 100 percent because of rounding errors.

TABLE 7.6
PTC Residents' Involvement in Programs Regarding Children

Extent of Involvement and Type of Programs	Number	Women Involved in Programs (%)	Women Interviewed (%)
Yes:			
Group counseling	19	37	19
Child development	18	35	18
Individual counseling	7	14	7
Nursery school	5	10	5
Not specified	2	4	2
Subtotal	51	--	51
No:	50	--	49
Total	101	100	100

the nursery school often worked more than the required number of hours each day to help set up and host special events such as art shows or evening open houses for parents and children. As for the limited enrollment of aides each year, both staff who work closely with the program and residents provided a variety of perspectives. For one thing, the pay is only 25¢ per hour and the number of hours for work is limited to weekday mornings. Some other institutional jobs pay slightly more, allow more hours for work, and may be more attractive to residents. Second, residents must be available during weekday mornings when children are at the institution. Many women are engaged in their own schooling at that time and are unable to participate. Third, the primary prerequisite for participation in the nursery school is completion of the child development course. As noted previously, many residents interviewed were not interested in taking this course. In addition, some minority residents disliked the fact that the nursery school was composed only of White middle-class children. They preferred to work with minority children. One Black mother who had not worked in the nursery school said, ''I would work there if there were Black children. Then I'd feel like I was making a contribution to the people.''

Staff and residents provided a number of suggestions to improve the child development course and nursery school program. Both staff and residents suggested that the school should be opened for both morning and afternoon or for summer sessions. In this way, more students and more residents could participate in the program. This suggestion, however, requires additional funds for supplies, teacher's salaries, etc. Some residents and staff also recommended opening the nursery school facilities to residents and their children on Saturday mornings. Many residents have visits at that time and could engage in meaningful learning activities with the children. A third suggestion was the involvement of minority group children in the nursery school. However, as the area surrounding the prison is predominantly White middle class, implementation of this suggestion may be difficult.

Special Visits

At the time of the study, regular visiting hours at PTC were from 1:15 P.M. to 4:15 P.M. on weekends for all residents. In addition, medium and minimum custody residents living on campus had visiting hours on Sunday morning from 9:00 A.M. to 11:00 A.M. and on Wednesday from 6:00 P.M. to 8:00 P.M.

Special visits refers to visits outside of regular visiting hours and must be arranged in advance through the unit supervisor. These visits are granted when visitors are unable to come to the institution during regular visiting hours. In addition, children may have special visits with their mothers (Purdy Treatment Center 1979:4-5). Although children may come for a special visit on any weekday, at the time of the study most special visits occurred on Wednesdays. Special visits could start as early as 9:00 A.M. and run through 4:00 P.M. Exceptions were sometimes made and children visited mothers in the institution as late as 8:00 P.M. From January through October 1979, mothers throughout PTC received an average of 113 visits from children each month (personal communique from Dorene Buckles, January 1980).

Of the mothers interviewed, slightly less than one-third (31 percent) had had special visits with their children since they arrived at the institution; the remaining mothers (69 percent) had not had any special visits. The most frequently given reasons for not having special visits revolved around problems in transportation or distance from the child's placement to the institution.

Many children lived across the mountains or in other states. Some mothers had had no contact at all with their children since incarceration. Some mothers thought their children were too old to come for the day, although the written policies for visits did not specify upper age limits for special visits. Only two mothers said they did not want their children to visit them in prison and one mother said that seeing her children on weekends was often enough (Table 7.7).

In terms of the frequency of special visits, slightly less than half (48 percent) of the mothers who had had any special visits had seen their children on a regular basis (every week; once or twice a month). The remaining mothers (52 percent) had seen their children whenever possible on an irregular basis— only once or twice since incarceration; twice a year every other month (Table 7.8).

In sum, special visits are an important way in which inmate-mothers may stay in touch with their children during incarceration. However, less than one-third of the mothers interviewed at PTC enjoyed any special visits, mainly because they could not arrange transportation for their children to the institution. Relatively few mothers did not want their children to visit them for a day at a time. Of the mother, who had had any special visits, slightly less

TABLE 7.7
Special Visits among PTC Mothers Interviewed

Special Visits	%	N
Yes:	31	(23)
No:		
Transportation	41	(31)
Child in another state	12	(9)
Not know child's whereabouts	8	(6)
Child too old	4	(3)
Not want child to visit prison	3	(2)
Sees child weekends	1	(1)
Subtotal	69	(52)
Total	100	(75)

TABLE 7.8
Frequency of Special Visits among PTC Mothers Interviewed

Frequency	Number	Mothers Having Special Visits (%)[1]	Mothers Interviewed (%)[2]
Regularly:			
Once or twice			
a month	6	26	8
Every week	5	22	7
Subtotal	11	48	15
Irregularly:			
Only once or	9	39	12
twice a year	2	9	3
Every other			
month	1	4	1
Subtotal	12	52	16
No special visits	52	--	69
Total	75	100	100

1. Percentages in this column are based on the 23 mothers interviewed who had had any special visits.
2. Percentages in this column are based on the 75 mothers interviewed.

than half had had them on a regular basis. These data suggest that, given the opportunity, mothers in prison want to spend time with their children. But practical considerations such as transportation or distance from the prison often preclude these visits.

Summary

The programs described in this chapter assist inmate-mothers and children to strengthen ties during incarceration. Conceptually and operationally, the programs share a number of common elements.

Conceptually, these programs uniformly recognize the importance of bond maintenance for inmate-mothers and children. Since mothers want to reunite with their children following release, it is imperative for them to have some basis for understanding one another and for developing a relationship prior to release. Similarly, the conceptual bases of the programs underscore the importance of enhancing parental responsibility prior to release. Although the philosophical underpinnings of many prisons echo the importance of independent thinking and responsibility among inmates, by their very nature, prisons tend to foster dependency. In this regard, programs to strengthen ties between inmate-mothers and children suggest one way to enhance an inmate's sense of responsibility. Operationally, inmate-mothers must take full charge of their children during the visits—feeding, grooming, and generally looking after children become the primary activities. Enabling those mothers who genuinely want to take care of their children and make decisions about their children's lives during incarceration, even intermittently, may go a long way towards cultivating realistic parenting attitudes, positive feelings about themselves, and a sense of responsibility.

A second common thread is the role these programs play in helping children understand their mother's current living situation. Children often worry about their mother's well-being during incarceration. Through these programs, the children may learn more about their mother's environment, where she is, what she is doing, and in some cases, why she is there. In this sense, the stereotypes of what has happened to mothers in prison may be diminished and both inmate-mothers and children may share their feelings and test one another in a structured environment.

A third common element is the mother's reactions towards these programs. These reactions provide an indication of their receptivity towards the programs. Mothers involved in these programs regarded them as helpful in understanding and in fostering relationships with children. The most helpful aspect of the program was the interactions with their own or others' children. In the nursery school, for example, mothers were rewarded by an opportunity to work with, guide, and shape children's behavior and to feel needed by others. The least helpful aspect of the program seemed to be the information provided in a classroom format. Mothers felt the least rewarded by reading about child care or parenting skills. In the absence of actual contact with children, mothers often were not involved in classes. Consequently, mothers unable to have children visit on MOLD weekends, for example, did not wish to participate in STEP. As noted previously, one drawback is that irregular contacts with children may lessen potential impacts of the programs to assist in bond maintenance. Therefore, provision of transportation is essential to maximize participation and possible benefits of the programs for mothers and children.

Finally, program administrators shared a common concern for liability with children in the prison. Liability is and should be a major issue for prison administrators when children enter the prison. In the present study, inmate-mothers usually signed waivers of liability. Although administrators were concerned for the safety and well-being of the children in the institution, none of them reported ever having a major incident in which children were hurt. Scraped knees or elbows sometimes occurred, but fears that children might suffer some major injuries were unfounded. Instead, children rarely fought with one another and the women generally expressed protective attitudes towards children of all ages. In addition, the behaviors and attitudes of incarcerated women around the children softened. Women often said that they "watched their language" and shielded children from behavior that might appear morally questionable. In this sense, the presence of children tended to bring out nurturing responses from mothers and nonmothers alike.[11] Taken collectively, these data suggest that inmate-mothers want to stay in touch with their children and that currently operational programs to strengthen ties provide beneficial ways to do so.

Notes

1. Furloughs or community-based corrections programs provide other means of visiting children outside the institution. Because of their custody status, rules and regulations or lack or formalized programs, most women in prison do not have these opportunities. Therefore, programs for inmate-mothers and children within institutions are very important.
2. These states included California, Washington state, New York, Minnesota, Tennessee, Nebraska and Kentucky. The federal system has more recently developed a program at the Federal Correctional Institution for Women, Alderson, West Virginia.
3. This figure was obtained by averaging the average daily population figures from November 1977 through June 1979. This information was obtained through the Kentucky Bureau of Corrections.
4. At the time of the study, 19 (68 percent) of the residents at DBCDC were White and the other 9 (32 percent) were Black. Of the total population, 18 (64 percent) of the residents had children under 18 years of age; 1 (4 percent) had children over 18 years and 9 (32 percent) had no children. For those women with children under 18, the average number of children per mother was 2.9. Only 3 women had more than four children. The average age of children was 7.6 years and 65 percent of the children were 10 years or younger.
5. Information for this section was provided by Jane Thompson, academic principal at KCIW, personal communique, 6 December 1983.
6. In addition, in 1980 a Family Visiting Program was begun within the perimeter of the facility. Inmates may visit over night with other family members. Frequently, inmate-mothers use this opportunity to visit with children (personal comunique from Sue Clark, superintendent of PTC, 7 January 1984).
7. Beginning in the fall of 1979, the child development instructor who began the school was no longer at Purdy Treatment Center. Given this change in staff, there may have been concommitant changes in the eligibility criteria or selection process. More specific information regarding the initial eligibility criteria or selection process were not available at the time of the study.
8. Interview with the nursery school teacher, Purdy Treatment Center, Gig Harbor, Washington, 2 June 1979.

9. At the time of the study there were 166 residents at the Purdy Treatment Center. Ninety-four (57 percent) of the residents were White and the remaining 72 (43 percent) were Black. Residents ranged in age from 18 to 52 with an average age of 29. About 115 (69 percent) of the residents were mothers with children 18 years or younger. The remaining 51 (31 percent) of the residents were nonmothers. The mothers had a total of 221 children or an average of about 2 children each. Approximately 65 percent of the children were 10 years old or younger. Of the 166 women housed at PTC at the time of the study, 61 percent (101) of the residents were interviewed. Seventy-five (74 percent) respondents were mothers and 26 (26 percent) were nonmothers.

10. The fact that only about half of the mothers interviewed reported involvement in some type of program to assist them in relating to children is somewhat surprising. Dorene Buckles, diagnostic administrator at PTC at the time of the study, indicated that the separation from family and loved ones group is required of all new residents. This group is designed to discuss the problems women face and to share their feelings about being away from those they love and other residents and with the counseling staff. The underlying assumption is that the women may feel more comfortable about their incarceration and the separation through discussions with other women facing similar problems. One explanation for the finding reported in the text is that mothers interviewed in the study may have forgotten about their participation in the separation group. Since women participate in this group for only a short time when they enter the institution, it is possible that any beneficial effects occur during and shortly after their involvement. Mothers interviewed in the study and been in prison for an average of about 18 months. During that time, there may have been other events that overshadowed the effects of the separation group. Another explanation for this finding is that participation in the separation group may not have had the intended salutary effects from the residents' standpoint. As Ms. Buckles put it, the women may "perceive the purpose of the group as something other than how staff see it, or just give credit to those services which were especially meaningful to them." The extent to which residents do not consider the separation group "especially meaningful" suggests a need to reexamine the purpose and actual as opposed to intended impacts of the group on its participants.

11. The same type of positive inmate response towards children has been reported elsewhere. Murton, for instance, noted that an inmate's newborn baby "was enthusiastically welcomed and proved to be the greatest morale booster I've ever seen in any institution." (Murton 1969:178).

8

A Unique Foster-Care Placement Program

As mentioned in chapter 4, children of inmate-mothers are most often placed with family members. Sometimes children are placed in foster care[1] because relatives are unavailable or unable to receive or care for them. Accurate estimates of the numbers of children of incarcerated mothers (or fathers) who have been placed in foster homes have never been compiled. Prior research suggests that only small proportions of these children are placed in foster care.[2]

For these mothers and children, the forced separation may be even more traumatic than for children placed with relatives because of the uncertainties surrounding foster placement. Other research on out-of-home placements indicates that these programs tend to generate a "pervasive and implicit anti-family bias" (Knitzer and Allen 1978:5). Parents are not encouraged to visit children, to maintain ties, or to meet caretakers; funds for services that might assist reunification of families are often unavailable; grievance mechanisms for parents or children are nonexistent and the massive amount of paperwork often precludes caseworkers from getting to know natural parents and their needs (Knitzer and Allen 1978:6–8). Foster care is only one such type of placement, and mothers in prison whose children are in foster care represent only one subset of mothers affected by the general inadequacies of out-of-home placements. The fact that their freedom of movement is curtailed tends to heighten pressures and frustrations still further.

Imprisoned mothers in this study whose children were placed in foster care often said that they did not know the whereabouts of their children and therefore could not even write letters. Some mothers were concerned that they would lose custody permanently; others felt that they would lose their children emotionally because they would become attached to foster parents. Discipline tactics frequently differed between foster and natural mothers who feared that they would be unable to handle their children after release. Still other mothers were concerned that daily care was inadequate in foster homes. They said that the children were sometimes dirty when they arrived for visits and could not be bathed in the prison. One child reportedly came to the prison with lice in his hair. In some ways, then, the concerns of imprisoned mothers about their children in foster care were borne out of their experience.

Yet even foster mothers who take meticulous care of children may be perceived hostilely by inmate-mothers. The lack of communication between foster and natural mothers can create tremendous barriers to dealing effectively with children. Moreover, an inmate-mother may not understand even the best intentions and motivations because she does not really know the foster mother's interests in the child and is jealous of day-to-day experiences with the child that she cannot have.

In addition to the mother's perspective, there are other factors that must be taken into account in considering foster-care placement for children of incarcerated women. From the standpoint of institutional treatment, inmate-mothers' responses to counseling may be adversely affected. A mother brooding over the care of her child may be less inclined to concentrate upon resolving her own personal problems. From the standpoint of the childcare caseworker, the adjustment of a child to foster placement may be affected negatively. A child who does not understand why he has been placed in foster care may think his mother has purposely abandoned him or may not respond favorably to the resources provided by caseworkers or foster parents (Buckles and Lafazia 1973:43–44).

Against this backdrop of problems surrounding the placement and care of children of inmate-mothers in foster homes, a few concerned staff at the Purdy Treatment Center for Women (PTC) began a program designed to assist bond maintenance between inmate-mothers and children in foster homes near the prison.

Prior work on inmate-mothers has mentioned the program (Stanton 1980:124), and there has been one article written describing the program shortly after it began (Buckles and Lafazia 1973). However, there has been little else written about it. Furthermore, there is little, if anything, written about the role and responsibilities of foster parents who care for the children of imprisoned parents.[3] Given the importance of the foster parents' role and their potential impact on the lives of inmate-mothers and their children, a clear understanding of their perspectives is warranted.

Questions of Interest

This chapter briefly describes the foster-care placement program at the PTC and the perceptions of foster parents participating in it at the time the study was done. Specific questions of interest include: How did the program begin? How does it operate? What changes in program operation have occurred since its inception, and why?

With respect to the involvement of foster parents, there are a number of questions: Why have foster parents agreed to care for the children of imprisoned mothers? How do they view their role and responsibilities towards these children and towards their mothers? What problems have they had in serving as foster parents for these children? How have these problems differed from those encountered with children whose mothers are not in prison? Finally, in light of the answers to the fore-going questions, what does all this information tell us about ways in which foster-care placements may be enhanced. Although the information gathered in this study is by no means a definitive evaluation, it is a first step in understanding this effort. Moreover, the program itself suggests ways in which current resources may be adapted to provide greater continuity in mother-child (parent-child) relationships during incarceration.[4]

The Foster-Care Placement Program

The Foster-Care Placement Program began at PTC in 1972. The program stemmed from discussion groups of inmate-mothers who focused on the problems they perceived in placing their children in foster care. In essence, the women had indicated that they lost confidence in themselves when their children were taken away. As one staff member who had been involved with the development of the program indicated:

> The child loses familiarity with the woman and the "super mom" image of the foster mother takes over. Often foster mothers and case workers make the women look like bad mothers. Women don't have the resources and can't live up to the abilities of the foster mothers. Children are raised in a way that is foreign to the mothers and the mothers automatically relinquish the children.

Within this context, the program was designed to place children in foster homes near the institution, presumably for the remainder of the woman's confinement. In this way, children would visit with the mothers more frequently than if they remained in placements far from the prison. In addition, theoretically, at least, the possibility exists for natural and foster mothers to meet one another and to discuss the problems, progress, and expectations for the child periodically. Thus, there is the potential for a smoother transition for the child from foster to natural mother once the woman is released from the institution.

The philosophical underpinnings of the program include several assumptions: (1) maternal care is a responsibility, not a privilege; (2) children should know where their mothers are and why they are there; (3) incarcerated women should not be deprived of their maternal rights; (4) a major portion of a woman's identity lies in her role as a mother and rehabilitation programs must consider this role (Buckles and Lafazia 1973:44–45). Briefly stated, the program works in the following manner. Through her counselor, an inmate-mother may request that her child be transferred to a foster home near the prison.[5] The counselor refers this request to the family and social therapist who discusses the matter with the child welfare worker in Pierce or Kitsap county. Caseworkers discuss the feasibility of the move with the inmate. For example, if the woman has but a few months to serve before release, the move may be impractical. Caseworkers then line up suitable foster parents and effect the transfer. At their own expense, foster parents bring the child for daylong visits with the mother in prison on a regular basis, usually twice a month. Since they live as far as twenty miles from the prison, their agreement to serve as foster parents for children of imprisoned mothers may entail a substantial investment not traditionally required of foster parents.

According to institutional staff, when the program was established, communication between foster and natural parents was encouraged. Prior to placement of the child, foster and natural mothers often met one another to decide whether or not the placement would be suitable. In addition, they often discussed mutual expectations for the child's well-being. This approach presumably created a partnership rather than the traditional adversarial relationship between foster and natural mothers and provided greater consistency in handling the child between caretakers. Moreover, continuous communication between the two mothers could lessen the child's success in "playing one mother against the other." However, as will be discussed, interviews indicated that the extent of involvement between foster and natural mother has been somewhat limited.

Shared decision making regarding the child's welfare throughout the duration of the placement could further enable the natural mother to maintain or perhaps enhance her confidence about resuming maternal responsibilities upon release. In this respect, foster mothers could serve as positive role models for some natural mothers.

Finally, when the program began, natural mothers, escorted by an institutional counselor, were able to visit their children in foster homes. This opportunity allowed natural mothers to relate to their children in their own living situation—to play and visit with the children in a more realistic environment than the prison setting. In addition, this contact reassured natural mothers that the living conditions of their children were healthful and comfortable. However, because of a change in departmental policy which now allows only minimum custody inmates outside the prison grounds, this aspect of the program has been eliminated for most inmate-mothers.

Foster parents willingly discussed why they had decided to become parents for children of imprisoned mothers; how they perceived their roles as foster parents for these children as opposed to other children; the problems they encountered in being foster parents for these children; and the extent to which they perceived the importance of a relationship with and responsibility towards the natural mothers in prison.

Background Characteristics of Foster Parents

The background characteristics of foster parents contrast sharply with those of inmate-mothers presented in Chapter 3. Foster parents were usually White, married, and about 43 years old. About half had a high school education and some had attended college. Foster fathers and a few foster mothers worked, primarily in blue-collar jobs. One foster mother had a day-care center in her home. Most foster mothers stayed at home to care for their own and foster children. Most foster parents had served in this capacity for two years, some for as long as fifteen years. At one time or another they had all had at least one child whose mother was in prison. Most of them also cared for children of nonimprisoned mothers. Thus, from their experiences they could provide insights as to possible differences in procedures when mothers are in prison.

The background characteristics of the foster parents interviewed are as follows:

1. Marital status: Twelve of the fifteen sets of foster parents were married; three were widowed.

2. Ages: The age range of the foster parents was from 24 to 69 for the women and from 30 to 57 for the men; the average age of the women was 42.7 and of the men, 47.5 years.

3. Education: Twenty percent of the mothers and 27 percent of the fathers had had some college; 47 percent of the mothers and 55 percent of the fathers had completed high school; and 33 percent of the mothers and 18 percent of the fathers had completed up through grade eleven.

4. Employment and income level: Ten (83 percent) foster fathers and three (20 percent) foster mothers were employed at the time of the study. Occupations included mainly blue collar work such as pipe fitter, policeman, truck driver, military, civil service, mail carrier, custodian, engineer's aid. In addition, one foster father was selfemployed, another was a furniture store supervisor and one foster mother did day care in her home. The average combined income was about $16,636 per year.

5. Involvement as foster parents: These parents had been foster parents for from 2 to 15 years, with an average of 5.9 years. Most foster parents had served in this capacity for 2 years. On the other hand, these parents had been foster parents for children whose mothers are in prison for from less than 1 to 5 years, with an average of 1.65 years; most foster parents had taken in children of incarcerated mothers for less than 1 year (7 people). For some parents, the current child was the only foster child of an incar-cerated mother that they had cared for.

6. Number of foster children: At the time of the study, the foster parents had a total of 47 children. Twenty-three (49 percent) of the children were their own, 7 (15 percent) were foster children whose mothers were currently in prison; 8 (17 percent) were children whose mothers had been in prison; and 9 (19 percent) were simply foster children whose mothers had not been and were not in prison. The children whose mothers are or had been in prison ranged in age from 8 months to 13 years. Some of the foster parents did not have any children whose mothers were in prison at the time of the study but they all had had such children at some time over the past few years. Over the past seven years, the foster parents had cared for a total of 31 foster children whose mothers were in prison. Twenty of these children had been in their care during the past two years.

The Decision to Become Foster Parents for Children of Imprisoned Mothers

None of the foster parents had decided beforehand to care for children of imprisoned mothers. Rather, a childcare caseworker asked if they would accept the child whose mother was in prison. Uniformly, for all of the parents interviewed, the mother's current living situation was irrelevant in their decision to accept the children. As one foster mother noted:

> I don't think it made any difference to us where the mother was. At the time we didn't have any children. . . . The caseworker called and said the boys needed a home. We decided to take them.

Another mother commented:

> We love children and didn't put any qualifications on the mother's living situation.

Still another mother noted:

> I wanted to be a foster mother because I thought that was the best way to give myself to someone else and get something in return. It doesn't matter if the mother is in prison.

Six of the foster parents had wanted to take babies or very young children and the children presented to them had mothers in prison. Foster parents often called these children "Purdy babies." Only one of the mothers reported initially that she had reservations about taking the child of an incarcerated offender because she didn't know what to expect from the woman's family. However, after she had talked with the mother, she felt that "women in prison are no different from anybody else."

Perceptions of the Role and Responsibilities as Foster Parents

For most foster parents, the primary emphasis was to provide stability, guidance, and direction for the children in the context of a loving, caring home environment regardless of where the parents were living. The foster parents perceived their main responsibility to be to the children and then to the inmate-mothers. They generally said that they treated the children of imprisoned mothers as they would their own or any other children. One mother noted: "They fit right in with our family. I treat them like my own children." Another foster mother said that "being a foster mother for these children means being a mother. I want to share love with these children as for any other children."

The foster parents did not view themselves as superior to or replacements for the imprisoned mothers but as temporary substitutes until the natural mothers could resume their role. Although children often called them as well as their natural mothers, mom, foster mothers usually made sure children knew the difference. One mother noted:

> I am a substitute mother while the mother is in prison. I am filling in for the real mother until she is able. What they (children) need most is love and discipline; they're insecure without it.

Another mother remarked: "My role is to support and care for these children until their parents can, which has been the case so far with all the children I've had." One foster father described the foster parents' role as follows:

> If the mother and children are close and have some relationship, the children have to see the mother. The foster parents are to make children aware that they are temporary parents. We are here to give you a place to stay, things to do, ways to make you happy while your mother's away. Your mother did wrong and she's paying for it. And then, when your mother gets out, you'll be with her—if things work out.

These foster parents did, however, note some major differences in caring for the children of imprisoned as opposed to nonimprisoned mothers. One difference commonly cited was that mothers in prison have less opportunity for contact with their children than other natural mothers. Consequently, taking the children to the prison was often seen as an added, yet welcomed, responsibility. One foster mother considered mothers in prison as

> more special. They can't go see the kids at will. So you should make sure the mother can see the children if possible. She may really resent the foster parents when she gets out if she doesn't see the kids.

Another foster mother commented:

> The main difference is that you have to go to prison and take the baby with you. That's different from what you normally do. But as far as affecting our feelings towards the child, it doesn't. For other children the caseworker would take the child to the parents. We would never have any contact with the parents.

Extent of Contact with Mothers in Prison

As suggested by the last comment, a second major difference noted in caring for the children of incarcerated as opposed to nonincarcerated mothers was the extent of contact with the natural mother. Most foster parents said that they had more contact with mothers in prison than with other natural mothers. Usually, they did not even meet the natural mother if she was not in prison. Contact between inmate-mothers and foster mothers was facilitated because most foster mothers brought children for visits.

Only four of the fifteen mothers said that caseworkers or sponsors brought children to the prison. Although not all foster mothers met imprisoned mothers, those that did said that they learned more about how she felt about the separation and what she was experiencing in prison. For instance, one foster mother said that after being "locked up with her, I could see what it was like to be a caged tiger." A foster mother who learned how other inmates viewed her as a foster parent described her visit to the prison as

> kind of strange. The first day one woman started cursing angrily. I asked [the natural mother] what I did wrong and she said, nothing. . . . I was nervous. She explained who to talk to and and not to talk to people unless they talk to you first. I am not like that. I like to say, Hi. . . . Some girls would come up to me and say, "Hi jive turkey. Why are you here?" Others would come up and say, hi. So it was unnerving.

> We'd talk in a corner and some women would watch. We didn't mind. [The natural mother] said that any new person they wouldn't like—especially a foster parent. To a lot of women out there, foster parents are bad people and they automatically have something bad against you. The minute they find out you are a foster parent they don't want a relationship.

Some foster mothers commented that, after they met the inmate-mother, they could see for themselves how much she actually cared about the well-being of her child. One foster couple said, "After we became acquainted with her, we found out how much she really cared for the baby. It made us feel better about the whole thing. We came to actually like her as a person." Although many of the foster mothers interviewed had met the natural mothers when they brought the children to the prison, only about half of the foster parents indicated that they had not talked extensively with the natural mother nor had discussed expectations for the child's upbringing with her. A few foster mothers indicated that they felt these discussions were unnecessary as they had learned enough about the child's background from the caseworker or other relatives. One mother remarked, "I never thought of it making any difference. Grandma told me everything. She wouldn't run her daughter down. But I just never got to know her." Another mother pointed out, "When I got him, the caseworker told me a lot about him. I just never thought of talking to his mother about it". Two other mothers indicated that no one had suggested that they discuss the child with its natural mother and that they never thought of it themselves.

A few mothers said that they had talked with natural mothers only once or twice right before or after they had taken the child. Sometimes meetings included caseworkers. Foster mothers indicated that these discussions were mostly small talk rather than discussions of expectations for raising the child. One foster mother characterized this first meeting as a way for the natural mother to "size me up." Another foster mother said, "We didn't talk about the future. We talked more about what they used to do and she told me something about herself."

Initial meetings between foster and natural mothers might be called by either one. Sometimes initial meetings were called by natural mothers. One foster mother said:

> The first meeting was called at the natural mother's request. She was mostly interested in how I'd react to her being in prison. Her child had been with another foster family for about a month and the foster mother got all worked up about her being in prison.

Sometimes initial meetings were called by foster mothers. One mother indicated that

> getting to know the natural mother was very important to me. I wanted to talk to her if she wanted to talk to me. . . . I wanted to know her feelings about the baby and about someone taking care of the baby. If she is afraid to talk to me about the baby, then maybe I can't do it. It is her baby. I know I take the responsibility but I want her to understand that if she wants to take her baby back, she can. I don't want to be in between her and her baby.

Perceived Responsibility towards Mothers in Prison

Although foster and natural mothers may have met once or twice at the outset, foster mothers reported that sustained contacts with natural mothers were not generally maintained. Interviews with foster mothers suggest that variations in the perceived responsibility towards the mother may have influenced the extent of contact.

Almost all of the foster mothers felt a responsibility towards the natural mother as well as towards the children. However, the extent of this responsibility varied. Some foster parents indicated that this responsibility entailed simply ensuring that the mother knows her child is receiving adequate care and affection. As one foster mother put it:

> My responsibility is first to the child and then to the mother to show her that we are caring for the child and raising the child as she would want it. We also want to let the woman know that we have respect for the natural parents.

For about half the foster parents, this responsibility involved establishing a relationship with the natural mother. Foster mothers who felt that a relationship was important sometimes visited the mothers in prison and brought items that were difficult to obtain, wrote letters, exchanged views on the child's growth and expectations for the child's development and welfare and, for a few mothers, retained a relationship with the natural mother after the child had left the foster home.

One foster mother suggested that the importance in establishing a relationship indicates to the mother "that her child is not being turned over to complete strangers." Another foster mother suggested that if she were in prison she would want to know as much about the family caring for her child as possible; thus she felt that she owed it to the mother to offer this information. Many foster parents indicated that getting to know the natural mother would provide valuable information about the child's background which might assist in understanding current behavior patterns. One foster couple took this a step further and commented that in dealing with the child's problems foster parents are dealing with those of the mother: "If you don't want to get involved with the parents, don't get involved with the child." For this foster couple, attempting to straighten out family relationships was seen as part of their overall responsibility.

One mother indicated the importance of developing a relationship with an inmate-mother prior to taking her baby. The inmate-mother was initially hostile to the foster parents who were to take her child at birth, because she grew up as a foster child and had been treated poorly. The baby was born two months prematurely. When the foster parents visited the inmate-mother in the hospital and expressed an interest in learning to care for the premature infant, they gained her confidence: "Meeting the mother at the hospital before the baby's birth, we got to know each other and avoided a lot of unnecessary jealousies before I took the baby. It was hard for her because she gave the baby up before she left the hospital." In this case, the foster and natural mothers maintained close ties even after the child had returned to the natural mother.

Several foster mothers indicated that they felt a strong bond with natural mothers of infants and wanted to help the mothers as much as possible to retain ties with their children. One common theme revealed through the interviews was that foster mothers sought to provide guidance for handling and feeding babies of inexperienced inmate-mothers. For example, one foster mother reported that the 26-year-old inmate-mother "didn't seem to know how to act around the baby. She felt awkward holding the baby and didn't know how or what to feed it. So she asked me and I showed her. . . . We got to be good friends. She even writes to me now about the baby." Determining the extent of the relationship may pose problems for some foster parents. One mother questioned the optimal level of involvement:

> How much should or could you do for this person that would be beneficial for her and her child? How much should you get her involved in your family? Should you invite her to be a part of your family? How much is my responsibility to the mother? There are no easy answers to these questions.

One set of foster parents candidly said that in the long run they had become far too involved with one inmate-mother. They had taken her child from birth and had cared for him for eighteen months. During that time, the natural mother had also become dependent upon them. She called them Mom and Dad and often called collect from the prison. Even after the baby was returned to her, she left the baby with them. For the foster parents, the real problem was that she continued to drink heavily and considered their suggestion that she seek professional counseling for her drinking problem as an attempt to take her child from her. These foster parents summarized their feelings in saying that "she took advantage of us."

Problems Encountered in Serving as Foster Parents for Children of Imprisoned Mothers

During the interviews, foster parents mentioned a number of problems they had encountered in caring for children of imprisoned mothers. Problem areas included the natural mother, the institution, and the children.

Problems with the Natural Mother. Some foster parents indicated that there were differences in child-rearing philosophies that affected their handling situations with children. For example, one foster mother had understood from the natural mother that she wanted her son and daughter to be raised in a morally upright manner. At the outset of the relationship the natural mother had been pleased that the girl, in her early teens, attended church regularly and was doing fairly well in school. However, after a while she wanted to date and to wear jeans to school more often than the foster mother liked. The natural mother agreed with the girl. The foster mother expressed concern over this as her own children lived within the rules but the foster children seemed outside of them. The children left abruptly shortly thereafter. The foster mother felt both concerned about the girl's welfare and somewhat hurt by the natural mother's response:

> We wanted to be friendly and helpful towards her and we wanted to understand what she wanted for the children and what we could do for the children. After a while things didn't seem to be good enough. They didn't feel we were doing good enough according to what she wanted. . . . Dating was one. She finally didn't want them too involved in church activities. . . . One of the real bad things is that we asked the girls to wear dresses at least twice a week to school. This really upset them really bad. . . . She and I discussed this several times. She disagreed with me. She thought they should wear anything they wanted. Knowing how we feel about our young people, we expect them to dress modestly. This is how young girls get in trouble as far as we are concerned—when they flaunt themselves. I realize that maybe we have stronger ideas than the mother about raising children, especially young ladies. . . . Towards the end it was hard to be supportive. I wanted to be supportive of the mother but it got kind of hard.

Another problem area mentioned was differences in feeding children. One foster mother indicated conflict over feeding the 8-month-old foster baby. During visits to the prison the mother insisted upon feeding the child, who had a cleft palate, with a spoon. The foster mother, who used a syringe to avoid getting food in the baby's tubes and causing an infection, noted: "When the baby came back from visiting her, she'd have an infection so I'd take her to the hospital to clear it up." The foster mother was somewhat irritated at the inmate-mother's behavior because of the adverse consequences for the baby. The natural mother, on the other hand, thought feeding the baby with a syringe was inhuman, perhaps without realizing fully the reasons for doing so. In this case, the foster and natural mothers had not met one another. Had they been able to sit down and discuss the problems, perhaps they would have reached an understanding.

One foster mother questioned whether the natural mother really wanted the responsibility of motherhood. For instance, she thought the natural mother might choose a career over her children. As she put it:

> Don't get me wrong. [She] loves her kids. But she loves her career and herself too. . . . One night she said "I don't know whether I am going to pick the kids or the career." I think she wanted to see my reaction. She knows that at the drop of a hat they could come back here.

Another foster mother believed the natural mother in prison was capable but afraid to take on the responsibility:

[She] would talk about furlough like it was the only thing she ever wanted and then she would mess up before it was time to get there—maybe because she was afraid of the responsibility. I really believe she loves [her son] but is afraid of taking the responsibility of him.

This mother had escaped three times from the prison. The foster mother commented on its impact on her son:

He just loves her. Sometimes he doesn't even want to come home. During the last few times he didn't want to come home. He wanted to stay longer and I was doing my best to encourage that because he was supposed to go with her. The sad part is that she builds him up to go with her and then she disappears. Then there he is wondering where his mama is. How does he feel? He doesn't say in so many words but I am sure he must feel hurt. . . . He is still waiting. She is supposed to come back. But that's the sad part; he is really anxious to go with her. He keeps asking if he can go to his mama's house. He really loves her and she really loves him.

For these foster mothers, then, there was some concern about the children's welfare once they returned to the natural mothers.

For the most part, foster parents said these problems were not insurmountable. Often, problems that occurred were ironed out through discussion. For instance, one foster mother had been concerned about the mother's seeming insensitivity to the child's sunburn, but discussion between the mothers straightened out the situation: "I was mad at her one day because the baby was sunburned. But it's probably because she just doesn't know. So I told her and that was fine."

Another foster mother indicated that their foster son had been playing "both ends against the middle." This problem was resolved through a meeting of the foster and natural mothers, the child caseworker and child in question:

At first the natural mother resented us. [He] would go out to the prison and say that lady [foster mother] did this or that or took this or that away. His mother would tell him to tell me that she said it was OK. It got to the point that he was telling her things I hadn't said. So I had her created as a witch and vice versa.

But then we had that meeting and I got to know her a lot better and got to be freer and asked her if I did something wrong or what did [he] say. We got to talk things out and [he] was right there so he couldn't play his trick again. He was playing both ends against the middle and that is a problem.

After this incident, the two mothers reportedly were able to discuss differences and resolved problems about the child more easily.

These examples suggest that the problems faced by foster and natural mothers often stemmed from two sources—differences in child rearing orientation and a lack of communication. In many cases where mothers were able to discuss issues, problems were more amenable to solution. This does not mean, of course, that establishing relationships between foster and natural mothers resolves all difficulties. On the contrary, as noted previously, some foster mothers indicated that they had been taken advantage of by natural mothers who had developed dependence on them. Yet, it does suggest that developing some contact and understanding between foster and natural mothers may facilitate caring for the child by reducing some of the uncertainties and hostilities of both mothers.

Problems Visiting the Institution. The problems in visiting the institution were mainly difficulties in gaining access to the prison. One mother became irritated because prison staff at the control desk often searched the baby's diaper bag when she visited.

> A couple of times they got really finicky about searching the baby's diaper bag. You have to bring in food for the baby and diapers enough to last for all day. If the seal was broken on a jar of food, it didn't go in. They opened up bottles of milk for the baby and tasted them. They opened up the tabs on the pampers and checked them and after awhile I got to be a little annoyed by it.

> Sometimes I considered it downright rude. Especially one particular woman who would always give me a hard time. I mean she would take the lining out of the diaper bag . . . and all this time you are holding the stuff and holding the baby who is trying to get to mommy on the other side of the locked door. You know, I mean, if she had ever found me bringing in anything I was told not to bring in I could understand her looking like that.

When this foster mother asked why her things were usually searched, the response simply was "procedure." I said, "Why is it procedure when I come in but it's not procedure with the guy in front of me here or the woman in back of me? They never gave me any answer."

Another response among foster parents was that they sometimes brought children to the prison only to be told that they were not allowed to have a visit. The most common reason cited was that the inmate-mother had not completed the paperwork for the visit on time. Foster parents said that they were not sure if the inmate-mother had purposely neglected to complete the required paperwork or if the institution had mislaid it. In any case, foster parents pointed out that the resulting inconvenience for them and disappointment for the child were disturbing. It was especially bothersome for foster parents who drove up to twenty miles each way with no reimbursement for gas mileage to learn that the visit was canceled.

Some foster mothers said that the prison would not tell the natural mother that they were unable to visit and the natural mother would be upset with the foster parents. One foster mother said:

> One complaint of mine is that there were two or three times that I just couldn't get out there on visitation day. Like one time the baby was sick and I didn't want to take him out or I didn't have a car . . . and they would not give her a message. So here she sits out there wondering where the baby is and they would not give her a message . . . . They wouldn't even tell her that the baby wasn't coming that day and she would sit there in a panic.

Since these foster parents felt that a relationship with the natural mother was important, they were as frustrated as the natural mother in being unable to communicate directly with her.

Some foster mothers indicated that they thought the visiting schedule had been arranged without consulting them. As one foster mother put it: "No one ever asked me if the days for the visit were convenient for me. It was always for the natural mother's convenience."

But despite the distances to the prison, and the expressed inconvenience, all of the foster parents who drove children to and from the prison said they would continue to do so as long as necessary. As one mother noted:

> It's hard for me, but he loves his mother and I want him to see her as much as possible while she is there or else he won't even know her when she gets out. That would be a terrible thing.

Another mother said:

> The [foster] mothers out there should make sure that the kids can see them whenever possible . . . . I feel like if I were in prison, if my kids didn't come to see me, I would resent the foster parents when I got out. Say I was in prison and my kids were out. The people I love the most are my family. I would have to love the people who love my family. When I got out I would feel kind of hurt. That's the whole thing right there.

Problems with Children. Through interviews with foster parents, two common themes emerged regarding problems with children. Children often came to the foster home with physical or emotional problems, and foster parents often encountered problems when children returned from prison visits. In terms of the first theme, problems mentioned among older children included bedwetting (and for one foster boy, wetting during the day), aggressive or destructive behavior, not getting along well with others, discipline, and withdrawal. Foster mothers usually attributed these problems to the lack of a stable environment. Most of the foster children had lived in several other homes before they had arrived at the interviewee's home.

Some of the foster mothers noted that with continuous patience they were able to change the child's outlook. One foster mother said that the baby she received had arrived

> undernourished. The baby was extremely inactive. He would just lay there. He was more petrified than anything else. . . . He had been fed skim milk. You could see it was an inadequate diet. You could tell that by looking at the baby he was undersized for his age and he looked really terrible. . . . He would eat every two hours all day and all night and then he "graduated." He couldn't eat very much at a time. He got so his mama hardly recognized him. She was really pleased.

Another foster mother reported that the 6-month-old baby who had already been in two other foster placements was very withdrawn for several months.

> The first week he was here I had to hold him. If anyone came into the room I had to hold him or he would cry. He may have been afraid that someone would take him away again. He wouldn't smile. I just held him on my lap and he wouldn't smile. It took months before he would open up. I didn't realize a child could be so insecure at that young age.

Still another mother reported that when the teenage girl she had agreed to care for arrived she acted rather wild at first:

> She was so smart. She would find little things to do that she knew I wouldn't like. Like she would break things and she wouldn't tell me. I would ask her the reason for it and she would say, "Because I know you don't like it." She was purposely trying to get on my nerves. After the first month and a half we all considered sending her back. Finally I said no. What if somebody would get her and not understand her at all?

> She tried striking back so many times. It may be because of what she had been through. She has moved around a lot since her mom was in prison. But with constant reassurance and guidance, over time, this young girl changed her bad habits.

Another foster mother had agreed to take a 4½ year old boy and an 11-year old girl for a mother in prison. Both children had lived in two other foster homes since the mother's incarceration. They generally had to learn to live more modestly and to share things:

> The little girl would say, "I don't like things this way and they will just have to be changed." She had been used to having the very best of everything. She

had to change everything—like eating—from what she had been used to. She had been used to eating steaks and that type of life—she had been used to eating a lot more of that than eating hamburgers and well-balanced meals. She gave me the impression that she had eaten quite expensively and, of course, we didn't eat that way. When you have a family you have to budget. . . . The children were used to having the best of everything—the best toys, the best clothes. They came with more expensive clothes and toys than the average foster child. . . . I would assume from talking that the types of offenses her mother and father were in for is how the children gained the extra expensive privileges and equipment.

The little girl was a bit haughty. My daughter was at home at the time and they shared a room. And she would say, "Now this is not the way it is going to be. It's going to be such and such." She had been the oldest child and was evidently used to having things her way. . . . But she soon learned to readjust. By talking with her she learned to share. You couldn't do it all at once. You had to do it a little at a time. The boy adjusted nicely. They both missed their mother. They thought the injustice was being done to their mother because she was in Purdy. . . . They thought she was innocent and that she shouldn't have been there to begin with. They felt their dad was not such a good person . . . that their mother was there because of his wrongdoing.

The second theme regarding problems with children was that foster mothers reported difficulties in handling children after daylong visits to the prison. The foster mother of one infant said that the baby sometimes acted "very nervously and would not allow anyone but me to hold him for the first few days after the visit." Four foster mothers said that the children returned from the prison tired and frustrated. One foster mother suggested that perhaps the child had felt insecure at the prison and had not taken time to rest. Another foster mother commented:

I don't think it was because she neglected the child, that he didn't get a nap, but that she just played him out. He was the kind that wanted to be napped in his own bed and there was no way she could have been better to him so when he came home he usually fell asleep from exhaustion.

Difficulties were encountered more often with older children. They were restless or unruly for a day or two after the visit. At first they questioned the foster mother's authority and then settled down again. One mother remarked:

It takes time for her to readjust because she is usually not disciplined when she goes out there. I guess it's because they [the mothers] don't feel they have the kids for very long. You can tell the difference. . . . When they come back they are a little more unruly.

In some cases, however, the rebellion is more difficult, as one foster mother noted:

> They get all upset after a visit. . . . I'm sure she let's them do what they want and I can understand why she would. But to have them come home, they are back to rules and regulations. They'd rebel. One time. . . . we went downtown to a restaurant just after they had come home. They were walking on top of the tables. They were just wild. . . . I turned around and they were walking on top of the tables, stepping on top of chairs and onto the floor. I took them outside and told them they could just behave or sit in the car and they were fine. But after each visit we go through this.

Two foster mothers indicated that the children sometimes brought bad language home with them after daylong visits at the prison. In handling the situation one foster mother said, "We tell him it is not nice to talk like that. Good boys don't talk like that and he is a good boy. In a day or so he usually stops." The other foster mother indicated that the boys had lately been correcting their real mother for her bad language.

This type of problem experienced with children following daylong visits suggests that changes in caretakers for even a day affects behavior patterns of children. The problem may be heightened by the fact that both caretakers are "mothers" for the child. Although they may not be able to verbalize it, children often react in ways which indicate their true feelings: defiance, aggressiveness, or withdrawal. The conclusion often reached by foster mothers as to the reasons for the child's behaviors is that, as one mother so aptly summarized it: "It renews in them that 'you are not my real mother and I don't have to do what you tell me to do'."

Summary

The Foster-Care Placement Program at the Purdy Treatment Center in Washington state is a unique way of enabling inmate-mothers and children to retain ties while mothers are in prison. Whether or not the program has been successful in a statistical evaluative sense is unclear. A formal evaluation has yet to be done. However, the information gathered in this study suggests that the program is a sound, useful alternative and has many strengths that should be recognized and could be replicated elsewhere.

The key to the program lies in the willingness of institutional staff, childcare caseworkers and foster parents to work together with inmate-mothers. Institutional staff and caseworkers initiated the program over and above their routine workloads and have sustained this effort for the past decade. They have volunteered time and resources to do the little things that make the program work, such as scheduling and meeting with foster parents and inmate-mothers, ensuring that children get to prison visits, sometimes bringing children to the prison themselves, making contacts with agencies across the state, doing paper work to transfer children, and finding appropriate foster placements near the prison.

Foster parents have willingly expended time and resources to bring children to the prison twice a month for daylong visits. This effort often entails driving twenty miles each way twice a day. For these foster parents, then, participation in this program involves an additional financial commitment beyond that required by traditional foster care. Some foster parents went out of their way to become better acquainted with mothers in prison. They visited the mothers in prison and discussed not only concerns about the child but also the uncertainties and problems inmate-mothers face during incarceration. These foster mothers reported gaining a greater sensitivity towards the conditions of confinement and its impact on inmate-mothers as people. Moreover, they said they could understand more fully how much inmate-mothers care for their children. Developing a relationship with inmate-mothers often enabled them to work through difficulties with the children more readily. Some foster mothers also served as positive role models, particularly for inmate-mothers with infants or very small children. They shared feeding and diapering techniques and often stayed in touch after mother's release to provide additional guidance if requested.

There are, however, a number of unresolved issues about the program. There is an obvious need for additional staff both within and outside the institution to handle the requests for transfers for children and to oversee the foster placements once they occur. Additional workloads for already overworked staff make it difficult to ensure efficient, effective care in handling each case. Second, there is a need within the institution to coordinate requests for daylong visits so foster parents do not needlessly bring children into the prison when visits have been cancelled. Similarly, if foster parents are unable to bring children for scheduled visits, there should be a means to let inmate-mothers know in order to minimize added uncertainties and hostilities misdirected towards foster parents or caseworkers.

Third, there is a need for guidelines to assist foster parents in determining for themselves the nature and extent of their involvement with and responsibility towards inmate-mothers. These guidelines may encourage reluctant foster parents to get to know inmate-mothers better and may assist others to curtail their involvement when it becomes too intense. A key element in the program is the communication between foster and natural mothers. Although problems do not simply disappear through discussion, communication dissipates fears and doubts, makes the separation more tolerable for inmate-mothers, and may give them a more favorable view of foster parents. Similarly, foster parents who get to know inmate-mothers better can learn more about the interest and potential of these mothers in resuming care of children upon release. Throughout the interviews, foster mothers who knew inmate-mothers cared about their children expressed concern that children return to the inmatemothers upon release rather than to some "stranger."

In addition, foster parents should be encouraged to take a tour and participate in an orientation about the institution before taking children of imprisoned mothers. This could be done in conjunction with an initial meeting of foster and natural mothers and childcare caseworkers at the prison. In this way, foster parents will better understand the institutional concerns about security and will have a firsthand look at the conditions of confinement for inmate-mothers.

Fourth, the involvement of childcare caseworkers in placing children near the prison should be emphasized for inmate-mothers. These women often view childcare caseworkers as "those people who are trying to take my baby," as many inmate-mothers put it. This perception had developed over time with some basis, in fact, because these caseworkers are often the ones who encourage inmate-mothers to relinquish children. Yet, in this truly nontraditional program, childcare caseworkers have a very different role: they bring children to the mothers. This involvement could well cast these workers in a different light for inmate-mothers. They may come to understand that caseworkers are interested and willing to assist them to keep their children if possible.

Finally, ideally, fathers should be involved in the placement process and in the visiting whenever possible. All too often, children of inmate-mothers have no fathers. However, those who do will presumably return to a two-parent family upon the mother's release. Therefore, developing family relationships during incarceration, to the extent possible, may reduce problems in the transition. The information presented in this chapter provides a glimpse of future possibilities to effect bond maintenance that should be explored further.

Notes

1. This Foster-Care Placement Program is not a program in the usual sense. There is no formal project director, no staff, and no line item in the budget. Rather, this program operates informally because of the collaborative efforts of a few very dedicated institutional staff at the Purdy Treatment Center and childcare caseworkers in the Department of Health and Human Services. I have used the term program in the title and text primarily to simplify discussion. Further, I have used the adjective unique in describing the program because at the time of the study, this was the only effort of its kind in the country. This program is a very "well-kept" secret.
2. In this study, of the 283 children, only 21 or 7.4 percent had been placed in foster care; other studies similarly indicate that few children of inmate-mothers are in foster care. Glick and Neto (1977:119) found that 14.5 percent of the children of women in her study wer in foster care or with friends and that women who have been living either alone or with a friend prior to imprisonment were more likely

to have placed their children in foster care. McGowan and Blumenthal (1978) found in their national mail survey that 12.1 percent of the 1,336 children who had been living with their mothers at the time of arrest were living in foster care during the study. In addition, only 2.7 percent of the children of women incarcerated in the New York City Correctional Institute for Women were living with foster parents at the time of the study. It is not surprising that there is little data on the number of children of incarcerated mothers in foster care. In general, data collection efforts relevant to children placed away from home have been described elsewhere as "grossly inadequate." Knitzer and Allen (1978:2) indicated that "no federal agency knows how many children are indeed in out-of-home care." Yet, based on fragmented data sets, the report estimated that from one-half to three-quarters of a million children lived in out-of-home placements. These placements might include foster homes, group homes, institutions, residential treatment centers, or special schools or hospitals.

3. There is very little written about foster parents in general. David Fanshel's recently completed study on the characteristics and parenting attitudes of a sample of foster parents points out that, prior to his work, research on foster parents had not been done since 1943 (Fanshel 1975:3). There has, however, been some work on issues in the placement of children in foster homes, particularly in terms of permanent placements (see, for example, Emlen et al. 1978, and Pike et al. 1977).

4. Information about the program was obtained through interviews with Purdy Treatment Center staff and childcare caseworkers from the Department of Social and Health Services in the two counties (Kitsap and Pierce) participating in the program. Foster parents were recruited with the assistance of institutional staff and caseworkers. Sixteen sets of names were provided; of these, 15 sets of foster parents (15 foster mothers and 3 foster fathers) agreed to be interviewed. The other foster mother was preparing to take vacation and was thus unavailable. Interviews lasted from two to four hours with an average of about three hours each. All interviews were conducted at foster parents' homes by the principal investigator during the summer of 1979. The interviewer explained the nature of the project, the purpose of the interviews, and requested foster parents to sign a consent form prior to participation. Throughout the interviews foster parents were encouraged to ask questions about the project. The data presented here are only part of those which were collected.

5. In Washington state, children placed in foster care may be either wards of the court or voluntary placements by consent. The difference lies in who has the authority to transfer. In the former, the court has legal authority for the child and thus grants or denies the request for transfer; in the latter, the woman retains legal custody and authority to request the transfer herself.

9

Implications of the Study: Where Do
We Go from Here?

The separation brought about by incarceration affects both mothers and children. The present exploratory study has examined some of the impacts from the mother's perspective. A number of conclusions may be drawn about the separation, programs to retain ties, directions for change, and issues that require further study.

Impacts of the Separation

As noted in Chapter 3, like most women in prison, mothers in prison tend to be primarily Black, undereducated, unskilled, unmarried, and unemployed at the time of arrest. For imprisoned mothers, one of the greatest punishments incarceration carries with it is the separation from their children. Separation is antithetical to the development of parental responsibility. As one mother put it, "I can do the time alone OK. But it's not knowing what's happening to my son that hurts the most."

The greatest involvement of inmate-mothers lies in the placement of children prior to incarceration. Mothers who were involved in determining placements expressed the most satisfaction with the placements. Beyond this involvement, however, the role that inmate-mothers play as parents is minimal. Children live outside the institution in the care of others who are directly responsible for their well-being. Mothers mentioned that sometimes caretakers elicited their opinions on minor matters such as haircutting. However, for more important issues like dating, smoking, or using drugs, mothers felt left out and consequently powerless to influence their children's lives.

Decisions regarding visitation are contingent upon the concurrence of caretakers. Mothers may want their children to visit but caretakers may be reluctant to encourage this contact or may be unable to provide transportation. Given these constraints, mothers expressed feelings of inadequacy, despondency, and fear of permanent loss of their children.

Furthermore, since their own behavior has caused the separation, most mothers feel a great deal of guilt and shame. Their behavior has disrupted their children's lives, as well as their own. For mothers who had been involved in drugs on the outside, this disruption may have begun months or even years before the current incarceration. The lack of contact engenders despondency and fear that regaining the confidence and respect of their children after release will be difficult. Mothers whose children are placed with nonrelatives additionally fear that they will lose their children altogether. Expressions of presumed confidence in resuming their role as mothers upon release thus belie the inner fears many mothers have of taking the responsibility for their children after release.

Despite these feelings of inadequacy, most mothers want to retain ties with children and resume parental responsibility after release. This conclusion stems from several findings presented in Chapter 4. First, mothers and children frequently lived together and independently from other family members prior to incarceration and, for most mothers and children, the current incarceration is the first major separation from one another.

Second, about half of the mothers retained legal custody of children during incarceration. Those mothers who relinquished custody voluntarily did so because they believed that their children would benefit more from a nonincarcerated guardian. Regardless of the conditions under which custody had been relinquished, mothers uniformly wanted to regain it upon release, though they feared that their status as ex-felons might make it difficult to do so.

Third, mothers generally wanted to be honest with their children in telling them the reasons for the separation. Most mothers, at some point following the offense or incarceration, conveyed to their children that they had done something and had to be punished. In this respect, mothers feel children who are capable of understanding have a right to know what has happened to them. Mothers who had not had the opportunity to explain their absence to the children worried that the children would lose respect for them.

Fourth, mothers generally used the means available to stay in touch with their children. These means usually include letters, phone calls, or infrequent, brief visits in the prison. When longer visits with children were possible, inmate-mothers wanted to use them, but often said that the distance from the child's placement or lack of transportation precluded them.

Finally, almost all mothers planned to reunite with their children following release. Although they anticipated some problems in readjusting to the maternal role, for the most part, the mothers in the study believed that they could overcome these problems with a minimum of difficulty on their own.

Taken collectively, these results indicate that, regardless of race, inmate-mothers want to stay in touch with their children during incarceration and that they want to reunite with their children upon release. Variations in the circumstances of the child's placement by race of mother noted in Chapter 4 suggest that certain problems may be more characteristic of one race than another. For instance, since White mothers more often than Black mothers have children placed with nonrelatives, these women may encounter additional problems in communicating with children or in regaining custody upon release. Programs designed to assist mothers and children in maintaining ties should take these variations into account in meeting the needs of inmate-mothers and children.

As Chapter 6 suggests, understanding the nature of the problems faced by inmate-mothers prior to incarceration and their relationships with their children is a crucial component in attempting to assist these women once they reach prison. Mothers who had been involved with drugs prior to incarceration face additional problems in the separation. Their habits intensify the guilt and shame while in prison. Their concern that they remain drug-free once they are released further heightens their fears of what might happen to them and to their children. Care must be taken in providing appropriate and adequate assistance to enable these women first to handle their drug involvement and only then to handle their relationships with their children.

Although inmate-mothers enthusiastically want to resume maternal responsibilities following release, the extent to which they will be prepared for this responsibility is questionable. Cut off from the day-to-day experiences of parenthood, inmate-mothers tend to see the mother role somewhat unrealistically. The profile of child-rearing attitudes presented in Chapter 5, for instance, suggests that inmate-mothers may be somewhat lax in their view of disciplining children. Moreover, they tend to be overprotective and to prefer indulging their children with the best things available. Interviews with these women confirmed their fears that they may not be able to command the respect required to be an effective authoritative figure because of the circumstances surrounding the separation and possible rejection by their children.

These concerns indicate that inmate-mothers need and want some guidance in reestablishing their parental role prior to release. Yet, many mothers deny this need, perhaps because of a stereotyped belief that women who are mothers naturally know (or should know) how to be ''good'' mothers without assistance from others. The problem, then, is to devise appropriate ways to assist inmate-mothers in strengthening ties with children, in developing a sense of self, and in alleviating their feelings of inadequacy as mothers.

Perhaps one of the most important ways in which the fears of inmate-mothers could be alleviated is through continuous contact between children and their mothers from the time of arrest through release from the institution and parole. As noted in Chapter 4, inmate-mothers often have little time to explain to their children what has happened and why they are going away. The first contact with children after arrest may not be for several weeks or months. Inmate-mothers said that they had the greatest concerns for the well-being of their children during this interval.

In attempting to promote mother-child bonds, the place to start is when mothers are arrested or in jail. The series of events following the crime and arrest are perhaps more traumatic for both mothers and children than imprisonment itself. No doubt both are left with scars and uneasy, vivid impressions. Thus, a liaison, perhaps a volunteer from the community working closely with the police and other correctional personnel could provide a vital link between mother and child during the first few hours or days after arrest. This liaison could ensure the placement of the child in a stable, caring environment that meets the mother's wishes and the child's best interests. Further, during incarceration, if it is possible to place the child in a foster home near the institution, this liaison could be instrumental in making the contact and assisting in the placement of the child.

Similarly, throughout the mother's incarceration, a liaison could make sure that the inmate-mother is in contact with her children on a regular basis and may assist in planning visits to the prison. Just prior to release, this liaison could work with institutional and parole personnel to ensure a smooth transition of the mother from the institution to the community and to her children. There is thus a need for volunteers from the community to fulfill this important function.

Programs to Retain Ties

The programs explored in this study provide some ways that inmate-mothers may retain ties with children and may begin to develop a parental identity. Daylong and overnight visitation programs enable inmate-mothers to share quiet moments as well as to discuss problems and the separation experience itself. However, parental responsibility entails involvement in making decisions about the welfare of children on a continuous basis. Even those inmate-mothers involved in currently operational programs considered in this study generally are not involved in these decisions. There is thus a need to extend programs to include inmate-mothers in decisions regarding their children beyond the prison walls.

The program described in the present study that comes closest to this involvement is the Foster-Care Placement Program in Washington state discussed in Chapter 8. Inmate-mothers may be involved in the selection of the foster mother and, to some extent, in determining how the child will be handled by the foster mother. Conceptually, at least, inmate and foster mothers may develop a bond of mutual concern for the child's welfare. The extent of communication between these two women may lessen the child's ability to play one mother against the other and may enable inmate-mothers to relax their concern that foster mothers are out to win their children away from them. Moreover, foster mothers may understand the plight of their incarcerated counterparts and serve as a liaison between them and their children. In this way, the children may feel less threatened by the change in caretakers when their mothers are imprisoned.

Depending upon the extent of involvement of inmate-mothers with their children during incarceration, they may be able to resume maternal responsibilities upon release with a minimum of difficulty. In this way, foster mothers serve as role models to assist inmate-mothers in understanding how to handle their children.

Theoretically, involvement of inmate-mothers in making decisions about the welfare of their children might be accomplished by enabling them to live together in prison. However, given the current nature of prisons in this country, housing children in them entails moral and practical questions that relate to the institution, the mother, and the child. In terms of issues facing prison administrators, an administrator's primary concerns are the security of the institution and the safety of the inmates and staff. Adding children to an institutional setting on a long-term basis may threaten a delicate equilibrium and poses several questions. Would the addition of children create security problems? How safe would children be in the prison environment? Additional staff may be required to ensure the security and safety of the children, yet tight budgets may preclude the addition of staff or longer shifts. Staff may also be concerned about the added responsibility they would face.

Over and above security considerations are the practical aspects of housing children. With already overcrowded prisons, where would the children sleep? How could mothers and their children have any privacy? Who would pay for the room and board of the child—the state or the mother? Where would the children attend school? How could adequate medical and dental care be assured for them? What is the upper age limit for children of each sex to live in prison? How long should they be allowed to stay in the prison? Should they live with inmate-mothers or inmate-fathers if both are incarcerated?

In addition to concerns facing prison administrators, the impacts of living in a prison on the children must be considered. For newborn babies, the development of a close, initial relationship between mother and child during the first year of life may overshadow the negative aspects of the prison environment. However, for older children, there are a number of unresolved issues. What impacts would the prison environment have on their psychological and moral development? How could living behind clanging doors and within the regimented schedule of counts three or more times a day affect the perceptions and development of a child? How would a child view his/her mother as an authoritative figure when she, too, must first and foremost abide by institutional rules? How would children maintain healthy relationships with other family members and peers on the outside when prisons are far from home? What kinds of values or perceptions of authority would children develop?

There are also questions related to the impacts of the child's perception of prison life on his/her subsequent growth and development: How would children view life in prison? The prisons visited in this study which had programs to strengthen ties generally looked very attractive. Would children then consider this environment as far more pleasant than they imagined from the media? Would this perception influence their thoughts of getting involved with crime because prison isn't that bad after all? Mothers in the study consistently said that they wanted their incarceration to serve as a warning for their children to avoid similar behavior patterns. To what extent do inmate-mothers successfully inculcate these warnings particularly within an aesthetically pleasing institutional environment?

Consideration must be given to the impacts on the inmate-mother as well. Would she be able to handle institutional demands and stresses while simultaneously attempting to raise a child? Would she even want her child to be raised in the prison environment? Would she feel that she portrays an adequate authoritative figure to her children? Would she feel comfortable in disciplining children? Would she be more inclined to take out her own frustrations on children? Would nonmothers tolerate children living with them? Would there be sufficient privacy for mothers and children and for nonmothers?

Although not exhaustive, these questions illustrate the complexity of the issues involved in deciding to house mothers and children behind prison walls. Clearly, the answers to them are not simple and they suggest that the current prison environment poses difficult problems for raising children, which must be considered by well-intentioned reformers bent on keeping mothers and children together on a continuous basis during incarceration. Research provides little comfort in resolving these issues since the impacts of prior efforts in which children have lived with mothers in a prison setting for any length of time in this country have never been assessed systematically.[1]

An Approach for Change

Currently operational programs such as those described in Chapters 7 and 8, bridge the gap by maintaining contact between inmate-mothers and children on a short-term basis. These programs provide realistic alternatives to traditional visits. Yet even more could be done. Programs conceivably could be developed beyond the prison walls.

The primary drawback to any prison program is the prison environment itself. Philosophically, prison administrators want to generate a sense of independence and responsibility among inmates. However, this philosophy is antithetical to prison operations, which of necessity focus on security. In reality, prisons foster dependence. Inmates are required to abide by an externally imposed schedule and rules governing all facets of their lives. What is needed is an environment conducive to personal growth and development. Within this environment, inmate-mothers must be given a chance to make meaningful decisions that affect their lives and those of their children.

Mothers who care about their children have a vested interest in their well-being. Using this vested interest as a way to enable inmate-mothers to develop a sense of responsibility may be the best means of rehabilitation available. However, in this country, giving incarcerated women real decision-making authority, particularly in matters concerning their children, has rarely been done.

Involvement in decisions about their children begins with the decision to be a mother. Inmate-mothers should be encouraged to determine individually whether or not they will remain involved with their children during and after incarceration. Some women may feel uncomfortable as mothers and may not want to be with their children. Yet, they may deny their true feelings to avoid being viewed by others as "bad mothers." Many of these women may, in fact, feel uncertain of their own abilities as mothers. Other women may feel constrained by social pressures to act like concerned mothers when they feel otherwise.

In conjunction with the decision to retain maternal ties, inmate-mothers should be involved in major decisions about their children made by childcare caseworkers or others, particularly if these decisions will affect subsequent resumption of responsibility for children following release. Once the decision to resume maternal responsibilities has been consciously made, inmate-mothers must be able to maintain contact with their children and develop parenting skills during incarceration. Parental responsibility entails more than simply hugging or showing children off during intermittent, infrequent visits. Unless inmate-mothers have the opportunity to interact with their children regularly for more than brief visits during incarceration, they will be unable to determine whether or not they can handle the demands of parenthood along with the demands of maintaining a stable job and of parole requirements after release.

Furthermore, inmate-mothers should be involved in the development, implementation, and operation of programs to retain ties with children. This involvement will give the women a vested interest in the program and will enhance their decision-making skills. From the very outset, inmate-mothers should be involved in determining the goals and scope of the program, selection criteria and process, rules, disciplinary procedures, and grievance mechanisms. As the program evolves, the women will learn to deal with problems and deficiencies in the program. Of course, each mother must first determine whether or not she wants to participate. She should jointly work with childcare caseworkers and institutional staff to determine the appropriateness and feasibility of her child's participation given such factors as her minimum sentence length, her child's age and current living situation. Involving inmate-mothers in determining the impacts of the program on their children is yet another way to provide these women with a meaningful decision-making voice.

For those women eligible for release, this type of program might best be provided in a community facility in which inmate-mothers and children may live together. An environment that is less security-oriented, conducive to the development of independence, and closer to community resources may enable inmate-mothers and children to develop a sense of self, to learn their own limitations, and to strengthen their relationship through continuous contact. Within this framework, inmate-mothers may thus more realistically plan for themselves and their children following release.

Researchable Issues

In addition to the impacts of the separation, the data indicate additional avenues of research. First, there is a need to document the impact of the separation on mothers and children from the time of arrest through release from incarceration. According to inmate-mothers in the present study, initial reactions of children who experienced the incident and/or the arrest procedures ranged from stunned silence to torrents of tears when they realized what was happening. One mother who had killed her husband's lover in her own home said that her two young children "just cried and cried" as police took her out the door. Another mother convicted of forgery said that her 9-year-old son defiantly stood there and "kept yelling, 'Stupid cops! Stupid cops!' "

Long-range impacts of these experiences on a child's subsequent development and attitudes towards their mothers, themselves, authority figures, and law and order concepts must be assessed. This information will enable practitioners to devise appropriate intervention strategies to lessen the negative consequences of the separation for both mothers and children at various points in the criminal justice process.

Second, there is a need to provide additional comparative analyses of the impacts of the separation by race and ethnic origin of mother. Understanding racial, ethnic, and cultural differences in the separation may prove instrumental in developing means to maximize assistance to mothers and children. If, as noted in Chapter 4, the extended-family concept accounts at least partially for racial differences in results, the implications of this concept for readjustment to maternal responsibilities should be examined. Programs to retain ties and assist readjustment may then capitalize on the positive aspects of the extended family. Moreover, the extended family may be more a product of cultural and ethnic rather than racial differences.

The extent that the extended family influences mother-child ties during and after incarceration as well as its influence on the mother's self-perception and general adjustment following release should be explored. Some of the questions to be raised are: To what extent does the extended family assist mothers and children in bond-maintenance during incarceration? Do those inmate-mothers who have an extended family return to a supportive social network which may assist in readjustment for both mothers and children? What characteristics of the extended family may be fruitfully utilized in designing programs to enhance bond-maintenance and readjustment of mothers and children after release?

Third, there is a need to determine long-term impacts of the separation on mothers and their children following the mothers' release from prison. One possibility is that mothers who say they will reunite with their children following release in fact do so. An alternative possibility is that the mothers may be released but do not resume care of their children. Research regarding postrelease relationships between mothers and their children is needed. If mothers generally do not reunite with their children, is it because they maintain a lifestyle inconsistent with resuming parenting responsibilities, or because there is an enormous amount of pressure in attempting to reestablish themselves in the community? Are there racial differences in proposed and actual reunions between inmate-mothers and their children following release?

Fourth, there is a need for careful evaluation to document the short- and long-range effectiveness of programs in assisting mothers to develop a positive self-image and to understand and relate to their children both during and following incarceration. Moreover, there is a need for information on the ways in which programs that strengthen ties influence the lives of these children outside of prison. Additional research is needed to underscore whether inmate-mothers and children reunite more frequently after involvement in these programs than a matched comparison group of inmate-mothers and children who did not participate.

With respect to programs such as the informal Foster-Care Placement Program, there is a need for more descriptive information about the program. For instance, when mothers are released from prison—do they, in fact, take back children who have stayed in foster homes near the prison more frequently than if they stayed elsewhere and had had little or no contact during incarceration? Limited prior research on caseworker, parent, and child interactions when children are removed from the home indicates that the proportion of children returning home is higher when there was frequent contact between parents and caseworkers (Knitzer and Allen 1978:24, n. 38). If foster and natural mothers stay in touch, is it reasonable to assume that their contact will also facilitate the return of the children to their natural mothers upon release? Under what conditions is the development of relationships between inmate- and foster mothers most appropriate and effective? What character-istics of foster and inmate-mothers would be conducive to establish a good working relationship? How much contact should be encouraged?

Finally, the discussion thus far has focused on the effects of the separation on inmate-mothers. There is an equally important need to determine the short- and long-term effects of the separation on incarcerated fathers and children. Our culture focuses on mothers as the primary child-rearing agent, but fathers also play a major role in family life, and many more fathers than mothers are imprisoned. Research regarding the impact of the separation on fathers at each point in the criminal justice process will provide practitioners with information to assist in developing program options for men.

As the pendulum swings further in the direction of punishment as the primary means of handling criminal offenders, there is the temptation to dismiss the development of programs to assist ties between mothers and children as unaffordable luxuries. Despite this philosophical shift over the past decade, there remains a need to sustain relationships during incarceration. This need is evidenced by the crowded visiting rooms in jails and prisons across the country. Given this need, reality-oriented programs designed to develop a positive sense of self, adequate parenting skills, and to encourage responsible decision making among inmate-mothers are not luxuries, but necessities.

Notes

1. There is evidence that earlier this century babies lived with mothers for at least a few weeks at the women's prison at Framingham, Massachusetts, and the Federal Women's Reformatory at Alderson, and currently, at the New York State Women's Prison at Bedford Hills. However, to date there has been no systematic attempt to evaluate the impacts of this living situation on mothers or children following their release. This lack of data points up the importance of conducting follow-up studies of mother-child relationships in currently operational programs.

Appendix A:
Methodology

Study Sites

When the project began, there were innovative programs for inmate-mothers and their children in prisons in seven states and the federal prison system. Ideally, it would have been advantageous to conduct the study in each of these states. However, given the limitations of time and personnel, two states, Washington and Kentucky, were selected for study.

Washington state was selected because of the diversity of programs for mothers and children which have been part of the institution since it opened. Kentucky was included because one of the prisons was new and had a program for women and children. Although the number of women involved in the program in this institution is very small, the entire institution could be easily included in the study. In addition, Kentucky has two institutions for women: at the time of the study one institution had a program for women and children and one did not.[1] Given a variety of differences between the populations of the two institutions, direct statistical comparisons of responses are not possible. However, interviews with women in both institutions provide qualitative impressionistic data about mothers' perceptions of the separation, in one institution with traditional approaches and one with more innovative approaches to stay in contact with children.

Respondent Groups

In each institution, the primary respondent group was imprisoned women, both mothers and nonmothers. In institutions that have parent-child programs, a small number of staff were also included. Staff members were interviewed primarily to learn about the development, implementation, operations, and possible problems in the programs. In Washington state, a small number of foster parents who live near the institution and have served as caretakers for the children of incarcerated mothers were interviewed.

Data Collection Instruments

Data collection instruments included two standardized instruments, the Tennessee Self Concept Scale (TSCS) and the Maryland Parent Attitude

Survey (MPAS), questionnaires developed for each respondent group, and taped interviews for mothers in prison and foster parents.

Standardizd Instruments. The TSCS and MPAS were completed by both women offenders and foster parents.

Tennessee Self Concept Scale. The TSCS is a 100-item self-administered scale consisting of 90 items that refer to the self-concept and 10 items taken from the MMPI Lie Scale. Two versions—a counseling and a clinical and research form—have been developed. The latter form was used in this study. Items fall into one of five general categories; "physical self," "moral self," "ethical self," "personal self," "family self" and "social self." These categories have been further subdivided into three areas: "self-identity," "self-acceptance," and "behavior." The resulting 5 × 3 matrix provides a variety of dimensions to consider in assessing the self-concept. Items are answered on a 5-point scale ranging from "completely false" to "completely true."

With respect to characteristics of the test, there seem to be no data on the internal consistency of the instrument. However, there has been some work done which indicates that the instrument has some reliability and validity. Crandall (1973) reports that, in one study, the test-retest reliability of the "total positive" score over a two-week period was .92 and the test-retest reliability for various subscores has ranged from .70 to .90. Bentler (1972) reports that test-retest reliabilities in the high .80s have been found. In addition, he reports a correlation of − .70 with the Taylor Manifest Anxiety Scale, thus providing some evidence for convergent validity.

In addition to the "total positive" score, other scores may be derived from the TSCS. These include: "variability," which reflects the amount of consistency from one aspect of self-perception to another; "self criticism, which indicates the extent an individual is willing to admit derogatory things about himself; a "true/false ratio," which suggests a measure of response set; "net conflict" scores, which reflect patterns of responses to positive and negative items; "empirical" scores, which are used to discriminate among various groups (psychotic from normal respondents); and "number of deviant signs," which is a summary score of the deviant feature across all of the other scores.

For purposes of this study, however, the most important score is the "total positive" score. The TSCS was selected for use in this study as it has been used with incarcerated women in other research (Fitts and Hamner 1969). There is thus a profile of the self-esteem of women in other institutions already available, against which to measure the scores obtained in the present study. In this way, a larger data base on the self-esteem of women in prison may be developed using a well-known standardized instrument.

The selection of this instrument for the study is based on a careful review of the literature, reviewers' analyses of various self-esteem measures (Buros

1972; Wylie 1961 and 1974; Weils and Marwell 1976), and, as noted above, the fact that this scale has been used with incarcerated women in other research.

Reviewers' assessments of the scale's utility vary. In his review of self esteem measures, Crandall presents seventeen self concept scales in "rough order of perceived overall quality." The TSCS was one of the "two recommended" scales, the other being a scale used to measure the self-esteem of children (Crandall 1973:57).

Perhaps the primary drawback of this scale was cited by Wylie (1974) in her review of the self concept literature. She points out that since several subscales are derived from the 100 items, these subscales may not be all independent of one another. Bentler (1972:151) echoes the deficiency and estimates that perhaps two or three independent dimensions may actually be derived from the scale. But since the scale will be used in the present study principally to determine an overall self concept rating, problems in the use of several subscales assume less importance.

Maryland Parent Attitude Survey. The MPAS was devised in the early 1960s by Dr. Donald Pumroy of the University of Maryland's Counseling and Personnel Services Department. The scale was designed to measure attitudes towards child-rearing while controlling for the social desirability of responses (Pumroy 1966). The problem of social desirability has been a drawback of other similar scales such as the Schaefer and Bell (1958) Parental Attitude Research Instrument (PARI).

In the development of the MPAS, ninety-five statement pairs were devised on the basis of the type of parent they represented and the distribution of responses of people asked to rate each statement separately according to how they thought a "good" parent would respond. The parent types included on the scale are: "indulgent" (a parent who showers the child with love and gifts, impulsively buys things for the child, and is relatively lax in discipline); "disciplinarian" (a parent who needs and expects obedience, explicitly states the rules, fairly metes out punishments, and constantly pushes the child to achieve beyond his or her ability and thus perhaps forces him or her to grow up early); "rejecting" (a parent who is overly hostile to the child, often punishes the child more because of his negative regard for the child than because of the behavior of the child); and "protective" (a parent who is overly cautious of dangerous aspects of situations the child may be in, often performs commonplace tasks for the child that he or she may be able to do alone if given the opportunity).

Items are paired by the type of parent they reflect and thus control for social desirability. For each of the 95 statements, the respondent selects the one that is most characteristic of himself. The test is scored by computing the number of items in each of the four categories that were selected.

The scale has been used in a number of research studies including the relationship between maternal attitudes and behavior (Brady 1969), the relationship between parental attitudes and internal-external locus of control (Davis and Phares 1969), and in a variety of research settings, including the study of orthodontics (Allen and Hodgson 1968). In an assessment of the scale, Tolor (1967) found that the scale did, in fact, control for social desirability as there were no significant relationships with the Marlowe Crowne Social Desirability Scale. In addition, he found that intercorrelations among the scales in predicted directions generally supported the rationale for the division of items into the four parent types.

Perhaps the major disadvantage of this scale is that, to my knowledge, it has never been used with a group of offenders. Therefore, the argument may be raised that the norms developed on a sample of "normal" individuals may not be applicable to an offender population. Despite this drawback, the use of this scale in an offender population provides an exciting opportunity to develop an additional data base.

Devised Instruments

In addition to these 2 standardized instruments, questionnaires were devised to obtain demographic information and to tap perceptions of various aspects of maintaining contact between inmate-mothers and their children. Devised written instruments were completed by all three respondent groups. Taped interviews were done with inmate-mothers and foster parents. Written questionnaires included information more directly amenable to statistical analysis. Taped interviews included qualitative information such as perceptions of or feelings about the separation or relationship with children.

Parenting Survey—Women Offenders. This questionnaire contained questions regarding background characteristics (age, race, marital status, educational level, vocational training, and occupational status prior to arrest); opinions as to the optimal type of contact between inmate-mothers and their children; level of confidence about being a mother after release; situational characteristics for each child (age; sex; caretaker; satisfaction with placement; children's problems since the mother's incarceration; frequency of visits; phone calls or letters; placement prior to the mother's incarceration; prior separations; current custody of children); plans for reunion with children and anticipated problems; perception of children's knowledge of where mother is and reasons to explain the absence; and who told the child where the mother is now.

Women Offenders—Taped Interviews. Taped interviews with mothers included qualitative information such as how mothers feel about and handle the separation; problems they see in the separation; how relationships with their children have been affected by the separation; where their children were at various points in the criminal justice process and their feelings about the children's care.

Women Offenders—Records Research. Data pertaining to prior and current offenses; county of conviction; sentence length; parole eligibility date; etc. were obtained through records research. In addition, background characteristics on women offenders who were not interviewed were obtained from records research. Thus, information regarding background and offense characteristics was obtained for all women in each institution at the time of the study.

Parenting Survey—Staff Questionnaire. The purposes of this questionnaire were to determine staff perceptions of the development, implementation, and nature of the programs in the institution to assist inmate-mothers in maintaining relationships with their children and to determine staff opinions of the optimal type of contact that should exist between inmate-mothers and their children.

Parenting Survey—Foster-Parents Questionnaire and Taped Interviews. Both the questionnaire and taped interview were designed to tap foster parents' perceptions of their roles and responsibilities towards the children of inmate-mothers; problems they have encountered in caring for foster children of incarcerated women; and their perceptions of the type of contact between inmate-mothers and their children that should be encouraged. In addition, written questionnaires included background characteristics (age, race, occupational and educational level).

Procedures

Research Agreements and Informed Consent

Clearances to conduct the study were obtained from the Bureau of Corrections in Kentucky, the Department of Social and Health Services in Washington state, and the superintendents in each of the three institutions. As part of the clearance process, agreements were made between the principal investigator and the Bureau of Corrections in Kentucky or the Department of Social and Health Services in Washington state to ensure anonymity of respondents and confidentiality of all information obtained through records research and interviews.

In addition to these agreements, informed consent forms for each respondent group were devised. Consent forms explained the nature and purposes of the project, described the types of questions to be asked and the respondent's role, emphasized the voluntary nature of the participation and the confidentiality of all information provided in the interview, and requested the reader's participation in the project.

Interview Process

Data were collected in Kentucky during the latter part of March and April 1979 and in Washington state between May and mid-June 1979. The principal investigator conducted the interviews in all three institutions.

In each institution the nature and purposes of the project were initially described to groups of residents. Residents were encouraged to ask the principal investigator questions about the project or about herself at any time prior to, during, or after the interview. This was done because the interviewer wanted to share information about herself with residents just as they shared information about themselves during the interview.

Residents were asked individually whether or not they wished to participate in the interview. Prior to participation the interviewer explained the purpose of the project again, emphasized that participation was voluntary, that all information would be confidential, and that the resident's name remain anonymous, and encouraged the resident to ask questions at any time. Both the interviewer and the resident then signed the consent form and the interview began.

Questionnaires were completed in the same order for each interview: the Women Offenders Parenting Survey, MPAS, TSCS and, for interested inmate-mothers, the taped interview. At the end of the interview residents were again asked if they had any questions and were thanked for their participation.

With the exception of some small groups of nonmothers interviewed in one Kentucky institution, all interviews were conducted individually. Individual interviews were conducted to maximize the dialogue between the interviewer and each respondent. Interviews lasted anywhere from forty-five minutes for nonmothers to three hours for some mothers. Usually interviews lasted one and one-half hours. The length of the interview was determined by how much information the resident wished to share about her relationship with her children and her perceptions of the separation. The same basic interview process was used with staff and foster parents. Interviews with staff usually lasted forty-five minutes to an hour and with foster parents one and one-half to three hours. Records research was done after interviews had been completed.

Note

1. As noted in Chapter 7, since the completion of this study, the other Kentucky prison for women has developed programs for mothers and children. A very creative staff member at the institution used the data presented in an earlier draft report as a needs assessment to enlist the aid of state and private groups in devising both a parenting and, more recently, an overnight visitation program.

Appendix B:
Tennessee Self Concept Scale Scores

In their monograph on delinquency, Fitts and Hamner (1969) reported the results of several studies of delinquents using the Tennessee Self Concept Scale (TSCS). Collapsing the scores across these groups, the authors found a general pattern of scores, suggesting a relatively low and somewhat confused self-concept. Two of the groups included women inmates in the Tennessee State Prison reported by Patton for 1968–69, and female delinquents in Florida reported by Richards for 1967. The study by Patton compared scores prior to and following involvement in a treatment program. These two groups provide a backdrop against which to roughly compare the results obtained in the present study.

Since characteristics of the groups used in developing the delinquent profile of selfconcept were not included in the original work, statistical comparisons between these data and the data from the present study are inappropriate. However, eyeballing the means and general configurations of the scores provide some interesting similarities and contrasts. Self-concept scores for both mothers and nonmothers in the present study were combined as there were no statistically significant differences between these two groups on scale scores.

In contrast with similarities in scores for previous studies, scores in the present study tend to be somewhat higher on such factors as "total positive" score, "identity," "accepts," "acts," "moral/ethical self," "personal self," "family self," and "social self." These scores suggest, as noted in the text, that women inmates in the present study tend to view themselves somewhat more positively than their counterparts in previous studies.

Similar scores across groups on the "self-criticism" dimension suggest that, like women inmates in previous studies, the women in the present study have a normal, healthy openness to speak negatively about themselves. On the other hand, the "true/false ratio" score suggests that, like women inmates in other studies, the women in this study tend to define themselves in terms of external rather than internal factors. They are better able to define themselves in terms of statements as to who they are rather than by eliminating or rejecting statements that do not describe them. In this sense, they tend to use external evidence to understand who they are. Moreover, the mean "total conflict" score, though slightly lower than in previous studies, indicates some contradiction and confusion in the self-perception of women inmates in the current study.

Taken collectively, these data suggest similarities in the extent of confusion, contradiction, and external orientation in self-definition between groups of women inmates in this and previous studies using the TSCS. However, the data suggest that despite the confusion, women inmates in the present study generally tend to feel more positively about themselves than their counterparts in previous research, and in this respect vary from the delinquent profile Fitts and Hamner describe (Fitts and Hamner 1969:6–15, 90–92).

For the interested reader who may wish to pursue further research on self concept using the TSCS for women inmates, the scores for each of the scales obtained in the present study along with the scores from the previous two studies are presented in the following table. The reader is referred to the Fitts and Hamner (1969) monograph for more details about the self concept profile for delinquents.

TABLE A.1
Means and Standard Deviations of TSCS for Incarcerated Women in Three Studies

TSCS SCORES	PATTON[1] (1968–69) Tennessee Women's Prison		RICHARD[1] (1967)		BAUNACH (1979) Washington State and Kentucky Women's Prisons
	Pre N=34	Post N = 34	Florida Female Delinq. N = 51	Tennessee Female Delinq. N = 51	N = 195
Self-criticism	39.0 5.3	37.0 4.8	39.0 7.8	35.0 6.5	35.0 5.6
True/false ratio	1.5 0.89	1.4 0.24	1.09 0.40	1.28 0.48	1.4 0.36
Total conflict	42.7 12.2	39.7 12.1	38.0 9.4	41.0 4.7	36.5 13.1
Total positive	303.6 50.8	311.9 39.8	303.0 27.9	313.0 24.0	330.2 41.2
Identity	111.2 18.9	114.5 14.7	116.0 11.9	117.0 10.9	121.1 14.5
Accepts	92.6 19.3	96.4 16.4	89.0 12.8	91.0 11.2	104.3 27.7
Acts	99.8 16.5	100.9 13.7	97.0 11.3	103.0 10.4	106.6 14.6
Physical self	62.0 10.7	64.9 8.6	68.0 8.1	68.0 8.1	66.7 9.7
Moral/ethical self	59.5 12.2	60.8 10.0	55.0 9.0	58.0 8.3	66.3 9.3
Personal self	57.4 12.6	59.7 9.5	57.0 7.5	59.0 6.5	64.3 10.0
Family self	60.7 14.4	62.3 13.5	58.0 12.0	62.0 9.6	65.8 12.9

TABLE A.1 *(continued)*

TSCS SCORES	PATTON[1] (1968-69) Tennessee Women's Prison		RICHARD[1] (1967)		BAUNACH (1979) Washington State and Kentucky Women's Prisons
	Pre N=34	Post N = 34	Florida Female Delinq. N = 51	Tennessee Female Delinq. N = 51	N = 195
Social self	63.9 9.5	64.2 9.1	62.0 8.6	63.0 7.2	66.5 9.1
Total variability	56.8 17.3	55.1 15.7	61.0 15.4	56.0 11.7	52.2 14.3
Distribution	122.5 31.1	110.0 31.5	116.0 30.2	117.0 24.2	117.5 33.4
Defensive positive	48.4 16.8	50.2 13.6	43.0 12.1	51.0 11.1	50.4 13.7
Psychotic score	51.0 6.4	51.0 6.5	50.0 7.2	52.0 7.4	51.2 7.8
Personality disorder	59.5 16.0	61.9 12.4	55.0 12.5	60.0 11.0	69.4 12.2
Neurotic score	70.0 15.2	72.5 13.4	67.0 10.0	77.0 7.4	78.7 12.8
Personality integration	5.7 3.1	7.0 3.1	5.0 3.4	7.0 9.9	7.6 3.6

1. Data for Richard and Patton were taken from Fitts and Hamner (1969:90–92). Only those scores also obtained in the present study are included here. The author gratefully acknowledges permission to reprint the data from Fitts and Hamner (1969).

Bibliography

Allen, Thomas K. and Hodgson, Edward. 1968. "The Use of Personality Measurements as a Determinant of Patient Cooperation in an Orthodontic Practice." *American Journal of Orthodontics* 54: 433–40.

Baunach, Phyllis Jo. 1975. "Women in Prison: A Christian Challenge." *Currents in Theology and Mission* 2 (October): 284–90.

Baunach, Phyllis Jo and Murton, Thomas O. 1973. "Women in Prison: An Awakening Minority." *Crime and Corrections* 1 (Fall): 4–12.

Beasley, Laura. Undated. "MOLD Program: Mother Offspring Life Development Adapted to a Minimum Security Correctional Institution for Women." Belleview, Ky.: Daniel Boone Career Development Center. Mimeographed.

Bentler, Peter M. 1972. "Tennessee Self Concept Scale." In *Seventh Mental Measurements Yearbook*, ed. Oscar K. Buros, pp. 155–56. Highland Park, N.J.: The Gryphon Press.

Bonfanti, Marcia, et al. 1974. "Enactment and Perception of Maternal Role of Incarcerated Mothers." Masters thesis. Louisiana State University.

Bowker, Lee H. 1978. *Women, Crime, and the Criminal Justice System*. Lexington, Mass.: Lexington Books.

Brady, Grace. 1969. "Relationship between Maternal Attitudes and Behavior." *Journal of Personality and Social Psychology* 2(3): 317–23.

Buckles, Dorene and Lafazia, Mary Ann. 1973. "Child Care for Mothers in Prison." In *Social Work Practices and Social Justice*, ed. Bernard Ross and Charles C. Shireman, pp. 43–50. Washington, D.C.: National Association of Social Workers.

Buros, Oscar K. 1972. "Tennessee Self Concept Scale." In *Seventh Mental Measurements Yearbook*, ed. Oscar K. Buros, pp. 364–70. Highland Park, N.J.: The Gryphon Press.

Burkhart, Kathryn. 1973. *Women in Prison*. Garden City, N.Y.: Doubleday.

Chapman, Roberta. 1978a. "Child Development and Growth: Curriculum Outline." Gig Harbor, Wash.: Purdy Treatment Center for Women. Mimeographed.

————1978b. "The Purdy Treatment Center Nursery School." Gig Harbor, Wash.: Purdy Treatment Center for Women. Mimeographed.

Colten, Mary Ellen. 1980. "A Comparison of Heroin-Addicted and Nonaddicted Mothers: Their Attitudes, Beliefs, and Parenting Experiences." Washington, D.C.: National Institute on Drug Abuse.

Crandall, Rick. 1973. "The Measurement of Self-Esteem and Related Constructs." In *Measures of Social Psychological Attitudes*, ed. John P. Robinson and Phillip R. Shaver, pp. 45–158. Ann Arbor, Mich.: Institute for Social Research.

Daniel Boone Career Development Center. 1979. Residents' Handbook. Belleview, Ky.: Daniel Boone Career Development Center. Mimeographed.

————1978. "Project Narrative Description: Problem Statement." Third year grant application. Belleview, Ky.: Daniel Boone Career Development Center. Mimeographed.

————Undated. "Second Year Grant." Belleview, Ky.: Daniel Boone Career Development Center. Mimeographed.

Davis, William L. and Phares, E. Jerry. 1969. "Parental Antecedents of Internal-External Control of Reinforcement." *Psychological Reports* 24(2): 427–36.

DuBose, Dorothy. 1975. "Problems of Children Whose Mothers are Imprisoned." New York: Institute of Women's Wrongs. Mimeographed.

Emlen, Arthur, et al. 1978. *Overcoming Barriers to Planning for Children in Foster Care*. Washington, D.C.: U.S. Department of Health, Education and Welfare.

Eyman, Joy. 1971. *Prisons for Women: A Practical Guide to Administrative Problems*. Springfield, Ill.: Charles Thomas.

Fanshel, David. 1975. *Toward More Understanding of Foster Parents*. San Francisco: Rand Research Associates.

File, Karen N.; McCahill, Thomas W.; and Savitz, Leonard D. 1974. "Narcotics Involvement and Female Criminality." *Addictive Diseases: An International Journal* 1(2): 177–88.

Fitts, William. 1965. *Tennessee Self Concept Scale Manual*. Nashville: Counselor Recordings and Tests.

Fitts, William, et al. 1971. *The Self Concept and Self Actualization* (Monograph #3). Nashville: Counselor Recordings and Tests.

Fitts, Williams and Hamner, William. 1969. *The Self Concept and Delinquency* (Monograph #1). Nashville: Counselor Recordings and Tests.

Glick, Ruth and Neto, Virginia. 1977. *National Study of Women's Correctional Programs*. Washington, D.C.: U.S. Government Printing Office.

Goffman, Erving. 1961. *Asylums*. Chicago: Aldine.

Goodman, Nancy and Price, Jean. 1967. *Studies of Female Offenders*. London: H. M. Stationary Office.

Hays, William L. 1966. *Statistics for Psychologists*. New York: Holt, Rinehart and Winston.

Henriques, Zelma Weston. 1981. *Imprisoned Mothers and Their Children*. Washington, D.C.: University Press of America.

Inciardi, James. 1980. "Women, Heroin and Property Crime." In *Women, Crime and Justice*, ed. Susan K. Datesman and Frank R. Scarpitti, pp. 214–22. New York: Oxford University Press.

James, Jennifer; Ogosho, Cathleen; and Wohl, Robbin W. 1979. "The Relationship between Female Criminality and Drug Use." *The International Journal of the Addictions* 14(2): 215–29.

Knitzer, Jane and Allen, Mary Lee. 1978. *Children without Homes*. Washington, D.C.: Children's Defense Fund.

LaPoint, Velma. 1977. *Child Development during Maternal Separation: Via Incarceration*. Washington, D.C.: National Institutes of Mental Health. Mimeographed.

Lundberg, Dorothy; Sheckley, Ann; and Voelkar, Therese. 1975. "An Exploration of the Feelings and Attitudes of Women Separated from Their Children Due to Incarceration." Masters thesis, Portland State University.

Markeley, Carson W. 1973. "Furlough Programs and Conjugal Visiting in Adult Correctional Institutions." *Federal Probation* 37 (March): 19–26.

McCord, Joan and McCord, William. 1958. "The Effects of Parental Role Model of Criminality." *Journal of Social Issues* 14:66–75.

McGowan, Brenda and Blumenthal, Karen. 1978. *Why Punish the Children?: A Study of Children of Women Prisoners*. Hacksensack, N.J.: National Council on Crime and Delinquency.

Miller, Brenda. 1980. "Drug Use and Criminality among Women in Detention." In *The Female Offender*, ed. Curt Taylor Griffiths and Margit Nance, pp. 271–88. British Columbia: Simon Fraser University.

Moerk, Ernst L. 1973. "Like Father Like Son: Imprisonment of Fathers and Psychological Adjustment of Sons." *Journal of Youth and Adolescence* 2(4): 303–12.

Murton, Thomas. 1969. *Accomplices to the Crime: The Arkansas Prison Scandal.* New York: Grove Press.

National Council on Crime and Delinquency. Undated. "An Overview of the Pleasanton Children's Center Program." San Francisco: National Council on Crime and Delinquency. Mimeographed.

National Legal Resource Center for Child Advocacy and Protection. 1982. "The Court's View: The Incarcerated Parent." *National Legal Resource Center for Child Advocacy and Protection Newsletter* 3(1):18.

Palmer, Richard. 1972. "The Prisoner-Mother and Her Child." *Capitol University Law Review* 1(1):122–44.

Pike, Victor, et al. 1977. *Permanent Planning for Children in Foster Care: A Handbook for Social Workers* Washington, D.C.: U.S. Department of Health, Education and Welfare.

Pumroy, Donald. 1966. "Maryland Parent Attitude Survey: A Research Instrument with Social Desirability Controlled." *Journal of Psychology* 64:73–78.

Purdy Treatment Center. 1979. *Policies and Procedures Section 1.05.00.* Gig Harbor, Wash.: Purdy Treatment Center. Mimeographed.

Robins, Lee A.; West, Patricia A.; and Herjanic, Barbara L. 1976. "Arrest and Delinquency in Two Generations: A Study of Black Urban Families and Their Children." *Journal of Child Psychiatry and Psychology* 16:125–40.

Sack, William H.; Seidler, Jack; and Thomas, Susan. 1976. "The Children of Imprisoned Parents: A Psychosocial Exploration." *American Journal of Orthopsychiatry* 46:618–28.

Savage, James. 1974. "Parental Imprisonment and Child Socialization." Washington, D.C.: Howard University Press. Mimeographed.

Schaefer, Earl S. and Bell, Richard W. 1958. "Development of a Parental Attitude Research Instrument." *Child Development* 29:339–61.

Shared Beginnings. 1980. "Update." San Francisco: Shared Beginnings. Mimeographed.

Shepard, Dean and Zemans, Eugene S. 1950. *Prison Babies.* Chicago: John Howard.

Shoeben, Edward J. 1949. "The Assessment of Parental Attitudes in Relation to Child Adjustment." *Genetic Psychology Monographs* 39:101–48.

Siegel, Sidney. 1956. *Non-Parametric Statistics.* New York: McGraw Hill.

Stanton, Ann. 1980. *When Mothers Go to Jail.* Lexington, Mass.: D.C. Heath.

Sykes, Gresham. 1958. *The Society of Captives.* Princeton: Princeton University Press.

Thomases, Lawrence. 1982. "New Program Offers Help to Women Prisoners." *The Americas Gazette* (15 November):1, 3.

Tolor, Alexander. 1967. "An Evaluation of the Maryland Parent Attitude Survey." *Journal of Psychology* 67:69–74.

Ward, David and Kassenbaum, Gene. 1965. *Women's Prison.* Chicago: Aldine.

Wells, L. Edward and Marwell, Gerald. 1976. *Self-Esteem: Its Conceptualization and Measurement.* Beverly Hills: Sage.

Wolfram, Essey. 1973. "Developing Values through Milieu Therapy." In *Social Work Practice and Social Justice*, ed. Bernard Ross and Charles Shireman, pp. 37–42. Washington, D.C.: National Association of Social Workers.

Wylie, Ruth C. 1961. *The Self Concept: A Critical Survey of Pertinent Research Literature.* Lincoln, Nebr.: University of Nebraska Press.
——1974. *The Self Concept: Volume I.* Lincoln, Nebr.: University of Nebraska Press.
Zalba, Serapio. 1964. *Women Prisoners and Their Families.* Sacramento: State of California Department of Social Welfare and Department of Corrections.

Index

Abandonment, child, 2–3
Age of inmate-mothers, 19, 22
Aid to Incarcerated Mothers (AIM), 76
Alderson, West Virginia: correctional facility at, 97n2, 130n
Allen, Mary Lee, 119n2
American Civil Liberties Union, 4
Attitudes of inmate-mothers about: child rearing, 14–15, 30–31, 51–58; foster care, 100–101; maternal role, 7, 8–9; mother-child relationship, 1, 6, 37–38, 48, 98n10. *See also* Contact during incarceration

Background characteristics: of foster parents, 103–4, 119n3; of inmate-mothers, 1, 19–27, 121; self-identity and, 54
Bedford Hills, New York: correctional facility at, 75, 130n
Bell, Richard W., 133
Bentler, Peter M., 132, 133
Blumenthal, Karen, 9, 11n1,n3,n4, 12n5, n6, 18n2, 119n2
Bonfanti, Marcia, 8–9, 11n1,n4, 12n5, n6, 18n2

California: data about inmate-mothers in, 18n3; intervention programs in, 11n1, 75–76; law about children living in prison, 4
Caretakers during incarceration, 29, 47–48. *See also* Foster care
Child Advocacy and Protection, National Legal Resource Center for, 3
Child care/rearing: during incarceration, 29, 47–48; inmate-mothers' attitudes about, 14–15, 30–31, 51–58. *See also* Custody, child; Foster care; Maternal role

Child development programs. *See* MOLD; Parenting programs; STEP
Children: effects of separation on, 4–5, 14; number of, 25–26; problems of, 14, 31–32, 45–47, 113–16; reaction to mother's use of drugs by, 63–70
Colten, Mary Ellen, 59
Connecticut, law about children living in prison, 4
Contact during incarceration, 6, 12n5, 106–7, 121, 122, 123–24. *See also* Visiting programs
Crandall, Rick, 132, 133
Crawford, Jacqueline, 78
Criminal records, prior, 22, 24–25, 27n2, n3, 49n1, 54, 57
Custody, child, 33–34, 48, 49, 50n2, 122. *See also* Foster care

DBCDC (Daniel Boone Career Development Center), 77–85, 97n4
Demographic characteristics of inmate-mothers, 1, 19–27
Drugs: children's reactions to mother's use of, 65–72; criminal record for, 25; effects of mother's use of, 63–70; mother-child relationship and, 15–16, 59–74, 123; motives for using, 60–63; self-identity and, 59–74
DuBose, Dorothy, 9, 11n3, 18n2
Earnings, inmate-mothers' prior, 21
Educational level of inmate-mothers, 19
Eyman, Joy, 9

Family: extended, 47–48, 128–129; importance of ties of, 9–10; self-identity and, 54–55

145

Index